World Scientific Series in
Energy and Environmental Finance – Vol. 1

COVID-19 Pandemic and Energy Markets

Commodity Markets, Cryptocurrencies and
Electricity Consumption under the COVID-19

World Scientific Series in Energy and Environmental Finance

Series Editor: Stephane Goutte *(CEMOTEV, Univ Versailles St Quentin en Yveline, Paris-Saclay, France & Vietnam National Univ, Vietnam)*

Published

World Scientific Series in
Energy and Environmental Finance – Vol. 1

COVID-19 Pandemic and Energy Markets

Commodity Markets, Cryptocurrencies and
Electricity Consumption under the COVID-19

editor

Khaled Guesmi

Center of Research for Energy and Climate Change (CRECC)
Paris School of Business, France

 **World Scientific**

NEW JERSEY · LONDON · SINGAPORE · BEIJING · SHANGHAI · HONG KONG · TAIPEI · CHENNAI · TOKYO

Published by

World Scientific Publishing Co. Pte. Ltd.
5 Toh Tuck Link, Singapore 596224
USA office: 27 Warren Street, Suite 401-402, Hackensack, NJ 07601
UK office: 57 Shelton Street, Covent Garden, London WC2H 9HE

Library of Congress Cataloging-in-Publication Data
Names: Guesmi, Khaled, editor.
Title: COVID-19 pandemic and energy markets : commodity markets,
    cryptocurrencies and electricity consumption under the COVID-19 /
    editor Khaled Guesmi, Paris School of Business, France.
Description: New Jersey : World Scientific, [2022] |
    Series: World Scientific series in energy and environmental finance ; vol. 1 |
    Includes bibliographical references and index.
Identifiers: LCCN 2021021070 | ISBN 9789811239601 (hardcover) |
    ISBN 9789811239618 (ebook) | ISBN 9789811239625 (ebook other)
Subjects: LCSH: Energy industries. | Energy consumption. |
    Cryptocurrencies. | COVID-19 (Disease)--Economic aspects.
Classification: LCC HD9502.A2 C685 2022 | DDC 333.79--dc23
LC record available at https://lccn.loc.gov/2021021070

British Library Cataloguing-in-Publication Data
A catalogue record for this book is available from the British Library.

For any available supplementary material, please visit
https://www.worldscientific.com/worldscibooks/10.1142/12351#t=suppl

Desk Editors: Balasubramanian Shanmugam/Sandhya Venkatesh

Typeset by Stallion Press
Email: enquiries@stallionpress.com

Printed in Singapore

Preface

Policy makers and investors in the energy markets have worn significant fluctuations in oil and gas prices in the past, most recently during the 2014/2015 oil price crash. However, the current circumstances are exceptional. The rising COVID-19 pandemic and the uncertainty in energy markets continue to stress the business cycle of the national and international economies. The IEA reported that energy demand globally will fall by 6% in 2020 (seven times the decline after the 2008 global financial crisis), with advanced economies forecast to see the largest failures.

The economy is really being impacted. It started with the price of oil falling dramatically. As of January 03, the price of a barrel of oil was $63.02. As of March 18, it was $ 26.35. Russia and OPEC did not agree to support the prices. Saudi Arabia unilaterally decided to increase its production. At the same time, RTE (Electricity Transport Network) recorded a 15% drop in electricity consumption on Wednesday March 18, 2020 compared to 2019. Internationally, gas consumption, starting with China (and Asia), has fallen. What is recorded at the French or Asian level for electricity and gas can be seen all over the world. Wholesale market prices for gas and electricity are plunging.

Several aspects of energy and climate risk management are analyzed, notably the exogenous crisis of COVID-19. What are the determinants of an effective green energy development strategy? What is the Impact of Multiple Vaccines on the Death Rate? What is the relationship between CO_2 emissions, crude oil, and natural gas prices? How to measure the impact of the COVID-19 pandemic on oil prices, CO_2 emissions, and stock market volatility? How to compare the role and the safe-haven properties of financial assets and cryptocurrencies under the COVID-19 crisis? What is the influence of electricity consumption on the residential sector?

To answer these questions, the authors carried out case studies in several countries (The United States, India, and MENA countries) and made international comparisons (developed and emergent economies). The aim of this book is to capture the significant impacts of the COVID-19 pandemic on global energy markets, energy resilience, the environment, and climate change. The book will also be a source of the contributions to energy science, technology, and policy in the mitigation of the pandemic crisis and will provide a platform to share the most recent ideas and innovations across the above sectors and enhance interdisciplinary research collaboration.

About the Editor

Dr. Khaled Guesmi is Director, Center of Research for Energy and Climate Change (CRECC) and Director of Research Department, Economics, Energy & Policy at Paris School of Business. He is also adjunct professor at Telfer School of Management, University of Canada. He undertakes research and lectures on empirical finance, applied time-series econometrics, and commodity markets. Dr. Guesmi obtained his HDR (Habilitation for Supervising Doctoral Research) in July 2015. He received his Ph.D. in Economics from the University Paris Nanterre in 2011 and his M.Sc. in Finance from Paris I University of Sorbonne in 2005. Previously, he served as Professor of Finance and Head of Environment, Climate Change and Energy Transition Chair at IPAG Business School, and in associate research positions at "EconomiX" laboratory at the University of Paris Ouest La Défense and "ERF" Economic Research Forum, Egypt. In 2003, Dr. Guesmi joined the UNESCO as a Research Manager, and in 2008, he joined *"Caisse de Dépôts et Consignations"* as a Financial Analyst.

Dr. Guesmi is the co-author of many books and has published articles in leading refereed journals. Furthermore, Dr. Guesmi currently serves as Associate Editor at *Finance Research Letters*, as international advisory board at *The International Spectator*. In addition, Khaled Guesmi is the founder of the *International Symposium on Energy and Finance Issues* and the Project Manager of European Commission's Horizon 2020 Program for Research and Innovation. This program has focused on new models of cooperation between the

EU and the south-eastern Mediterranean region, which are expected to promote a radical redesign of these countries' energy strategies, focusing on sustainability and efficiency policies. Cooperation, for instance, could be applied to various aspects of the energy sector, including development of renewables, energy efficiency technologies, and demand-side policies. Sustainability and efficiency are certainly the domains where EU support for these countries could bring added value.

Dr. Khaled Guesmi applies modern financial econometrics tools to examine a broad set of topics related to the commodities markets. His research includes topics such as finalization of commodities and contagion effect between stock markets and energy markets. Dr. Khaled Guesmi won the award for the 4th best world researcher in *Energy Finance: Frontiers and Future Development* in Beijing in 2018.

About the Authors

Dr. Aida Allaya is an assistant Professor of Management at the Carthage Business School (CBS). She holds a PhD in management from Faculty of Economics and Management (FSEG Tunis). Before joining CBS, she held faculty positions at the higher business studies of Sousse (IHEC SOUSSE). Her research interests include Cross-cultural and international joint-venture performance. Dr Allaya taught a variety of courses such as principle of management, international management, and fundamentals of management.

Dr. Donia Aloui has a PHD in MBS-models, methods, and algorithms from Communauté Université Grenoble Alpes, France, and a Ph.D. in Finance from ISG de Tunis, Tunisia. She is an assistant professor of Quantitative Methods at CBS Business School of Tunisia.

Her research focuses on several topics such as Energy market fluctuations, climate change effects on financial system, investors behaviors on financial markets, Quantitative easing policy, the yield curve, Bayesian time-varying models, factor models dynamics, FAVAR models.

Sonia Arsi holds a PhD (finance) from IHEC Carthage, Tunisia. She is currently an Assistant Professor of finance at Carthage Business School, University of Tunis Carthage; she teaches topics of international finance, asset pricing, corporate finance, and treasury management. Her research interests include behavioral finance, derivatives, commodities, and international finance.

Dr. Ilhem Barboura holds an MSc in Biological Sciences from The Higher Institute of Biotechnology of Monastir, University of Monastir, Tunisia (2004), a Master's degree in human genome (2007), and a

PhD in Biological Sciences and biotechnology from The Higher Institute of Biotechnology of Monastir, University of Monastir, Tunisia (2014).

Since September 2008, she has served as an Assistant of Biological Sciences and biotechnology at the higher school of health sciences and techniques of Sousse, University of Sousse, Tunisia (until now).

She also served in the position of member of the ESSTSS Fundamental Sciences Committee since September 2013 and President of the scientific committee of the scientific association for health sciences "A3S" since May 2014.

In September (2014), she joined the post of Director at the Private Higher Institute of Nursing Sciences of Sousse, Tunisia. She served as a Director of Studies and Internships at the same university (2015). She also has two badges relating to C1 and C2 skills as part of distance education training (UVT) Moodle, Tutoring, Coselearn on March 4, 2015 at the Faculty of Medicine of Sousse.

Dr. Ilhem Barboura is a researcher in neurodegenerative pathologies. Her research areas concern biochemical and molecular study of Krabbe's disease, metachromatic leukodystrophy, Alzheimer's disease, etc.

Hana Belhadj is currently a doctor in finance from the University of Sfax. Her thesis title is "Bitcoin and gold as havens and diversification factors for developed and emerging markets: An international perspective of the COVID19 pandemic". Currently, she is a graduate teaching assistant in the department and has spoken at a number of conferences on finance. She can be contacted at: belhadjhana1@gmail.com.

Dr. Sahbi Farhani holds an MSc in Statistics Applied to Management from the Higher Institute of Management of Sousse, University of Sousse, Tunisia (2009), and a PhD in Economic Sciences from the Faculty of Economic Sciences and Management of Tunis, University of Tunis El Manar, Tunisia (2017).

In September 2020, he was appointed as an Assistant Professor of Quantitative Methods at the Higher Institute of Finance and Taxation of Sousse, University of Sousse, Tunisia.

Between April 2019 and September 2020, he joined the post of Director at the Private Faculty of Management and Sciences of Administration Sousse (FMSA Sousse), Tunisia.

Between August 2017 and July 2018, he joined the Private High School of Economics and Management of Sousse, the Private University of Sousse, Tunisia as a General Director. Previously, he served as a Director of Studies and Internships at the same university (September 2016–August 2017). He also served the position of Assistant professor of Quantitative Methods and Head of Department (October 2014–August 2018) at The Private University of Sousse, and Research-assistant of Quantitative Methods at the Faculty of Pharmacy of Monastir, University of Monastir, Tunisia (October 2010–September 2015).

Dr. Sahbi Farhani is also a Non-Resident Researcher at the IPAG Business School, Paris, France (since January 2014), and a Visiting researcher at the University of Lille 3, France (since March 2015).

Dr. Sahbi Farhani is a researcher in Energy Economics and Econometrics. His research areas concern energy economics, environmental degree of pollution, and climate change. His articles are published in refereed journals such as *Energy Policy, Energy, Renewable and Sustainable Energy Reviews, Journal of Energy and Development, International Journal of Energy Sector Management, Environmental Science and Pollution Research, Economic Modelling, Structural Change and Economic Dynamics,* etc.

Dr. Imen Gam holds an MSc in Statistics Applied to Management from the Higher Institute of Management of Sousse, University of Sousse, Tunisia (2009), and a PhD in Economic Sciences from the Faculty of Economic Sciences and Management of Sousse, University of Sousse, Tunisia (2017).

In September 2013, she was appointed as an Assistant of Quantitative Methods at National Engineering School of Gabes, University of Gabes, Tunisia, and in September 2018, she was appointed as an Assistant Professor of Quantitative Methods at Higher Institute of Business Administration of Sfax, University of Sfax, Tunisia.

Dr. Imen Gam is a researcher in Sustainable Development, Energy Economics and Econometrics at LAboratory of the Management of Innovation and Sustainable Development (LAMIDED), University of Sousse, Tunisia. Her research areas concern energy economics, water management, and Poverty. Her articles are published in refereed journals such as *Energy Policy, International Journal of Energy Economics and Policy*, and *International Journal of Advances in Management and Economics*.

John W. Goodell is a Professor in the College of Business of The University of Akron. His research interests focus on the impact on financial systems of national culture and institutions. In 2011, he received the Stockholm School of Economics/Women in the Academy of International Business Award for Increased Gender Awareness in International Business Research. His research has recently been highlighted in numerous media outlets including the *Washington Post, PBS NewsHour*, and *Bloomberg Businessweek*, as well as the blogs of the Columbia University and Duke University law schools. He is currently Editor-in-Chief of Elsevier's *Research in International Business and Finance*; as well as an Associate Editor for several leading finance journals. He is frequently invited to speak at international conferences and events.

Stéphane Goutte has two PhDs, one in Mathematics and one in Economics. He is Full Professor at CEMOTEV, Université Paris-Saclay, France. He is adjunct professor at University of Calgary, Canada. He received his Habilitation for Supervising Scientific Research (HDR) in 2017 at University Paris Dauphine. He is an Editor of Energy Policy (JEPO), a Senior Editor of Finance Research Letters (FLR); an Associate Editor of International Review of Financial Analysis (IRFA) and Research in International Business and Finance (RIBAF); a Subject Editor of *Journal of International Financial Markets, Institutions and Money (JIFMIM)*. His interests lie in the area of mathematical finance and econometric applied in energy or commodities. He has published more than 50 research papers in international peer-reviewed journals. He has also been a Guest Editor of various special issues of international peer-reviewed journals and Editor of many handbooks.

Salah Ben Hamad is a professor of financial and accounting methods at the University of Tunis El Manar. Doctor in Management Sciences from the Faculty of Economics and Management of Tunis, El Manar University, he also holds the authorization for research in management science.

He was director of the institute of informatics and management of Kairouan and of the IHEC of Sfax.

An international consultant, he regularly speaks in finance and entrepreneurship seminars. He participates in the evaluation committee for training programs in university establishments.

He is the author of numerous academic articles, co-author of several proceedings and of two books: *Contemporary Finance, Analysis, Evaluation and Applications*, at Economica, 2002 and *International Financial Management, Corrected Synthesis Exercises and Cases* at IHE Editions, 2005. He can be contacted at: benhamad_salah@yahoo.fr

Dr. Rafla Hchaichi is an assistant professor in Economics at University Tunis Carthage, Carthage business school, and affiliate at ESCTRA lab IHEC Carthage, Tunisia. She holds a Ph.D. in Economics from Faculty of Economics and Management of Tunis Manar and she has a Master's in finance and economic development. She undertakes research on public governance particularly public economics, bureaucracy, public choice, as well as new public management and total quality management. Her research includes topics such as cryptocurrency, energy, environment, climate change, and commodity market.

Soumaya Ben Khelifa is Assistant Professor in Finance at Carthage Business School, University of Tunis Carthage. She received her PhD in Finance from IHEC Carthage, Tunisia, in 2016. Her areas of research are Asset Pricing, Hedge Funds, International Finance, Market Finance, Financial Inclusion, and Energy Market.

Hela Mzoughi is currently a PhD and Assistant Professor at Carthage Business School, University of Tunis Carthage. She earned her PhD in Management from Higher Management Science of Sousse in January 2016 and she is specialized in Quantitative methods. Her Master's Research degree is in Actuarial Sciences and Finance from High Commercial Studies Institute of Sousse. Her research interests are quantitative finance, risk management, and actuarial science.

Sihem Ben Saad is an Assistant Professor of Marketing at the Carthage Business School of the University of Tunis Carthage (UTC), Tunisia. She holds a Ph.D. degree in Marketing from the Institute of Higher Business Studies of Carthage (IHEC Carthage). Before joining UTC, she held faculty positions at the Higher School of

Communications of Tunis (Supcom Tunis), Higher Institute of Computer Science (ISI Tunis), and Higher Institute of Technological Studies of Communications of Tunis (ISET'COM). Her research interests include digital marketing and child behavior. Dr. Ben Saad taught a variety of courses such as introduction to marketing, consumer behavior, project management, entrepreneurship, and corporate culture. She presented papers at several national and international conferences such as the French Association of Marketing (AFM) and the Tunisian Association of Marketing (ATM).

Fayda Taârit has a PhD in Economy from the University of Tunis El Manar, Tunisia. She is Professor of Micro economy and Macro economy. Her research interests are at the intersection of Banking Productivity and Information Technology. She works in that and other areas, monetary policy and financial fragility.

Christian Urom is in the last year of his doctoral training in economics at Laboratoire d'Economie Dionysien (LED), Universite' Paris VIII. Christian is a Research Assistant, Center of Research for Energy and Climate Change (CRECC), Paris School of Business, Paris, France. He received his M.Sc. in International Economics and Finance from Glasgow Caledonian University, Glasgow, United Kingdom. Previously, he served as a Research Fellow, Applied Economics unit, Afriheritage institution and as credit Advisor, Mutual Benefits Assurance group. Christian has over seven years of teaching and research experience in economics and finance. His research interests are in energy economics, asset pricing, commodity finance, and climate change. Christian has published in leading peer-reviewed journals including *International Economics*, *Energy Economics*, and *Economic Modelling*.

Contents

Chapter 1

The Impact of Multiple Vaccines on the Death Rate — A Focused Review for BCG Vaccination in the COVID-19 Pandemic Period

Sahbi Farhani[*,†,**], Imen Gam[‡,§,††], and
Ilhem Barboura[¶,|,‡‡]

[*]*QUARG UR17ES26, ESCT, Campus University of Manouba,
2010, Manouba, Tunisia*
[†]*Higher Institute of Finance and Taxation of Sousse,
University of Sousse, Sousse, Tunisia*
[‡]*LAMIDED Laboratory, ISG Sousse, University of Sousse,
Sousse, Tunisia*
[§]*Higher Institute of Business Administration of Sfax,
University of Sfax, Sfax, Tunisia*
[¶]*Biochemistry Laboratory, CHU Farhat Hached, Sousse,
Tunisia*
[|]*Higher School of Health Sciences and Techniques,
University of Sousse, Sousse, Tunisia*
[**]*sahbi.farhani@isffs.u-sousse.tn*
[††]*imen.gam@isaas.usf.tn*
[‡‡]*ilhembarboura@esstsso.u-sousse.tn*

Like other infectious diseases, controlling COVID-19 infection must be a priority in order to save all of humanity. In absence of a specific vaccination against the novel 2019 coronavirus, many researchers suggest that Bacillus Calmette–Guérin (BCG) vaccination can boost the human immunity system and have a protective effect against this infection. In this study, we use two methods: Analysis of Covariance (ANCOVA) and

Ordinary Least Squares (OLS) regression in order to explore the role of existing vaccines on COVID-19 mortality. Results are very promising and interesting. In fact, contrary to the emerging intuition, we prove that BCG vaccination does not have a relevant impact on COVID-19 mortality numbers. In this regards, another contribution of our chapter is showing that other vaccines could be paid more attention, as Hepatitis B of Adults (HepB1), Varicella-Zoster (VZ), and especially, Meningococcal C conjugate (MenC) vaccines have a negative impact on COVID-19 mortality in contrast to Diphtheria and Tetanus Toxoids (DT) Vac-Cube for older children/adults.

Keywords: COVID-19, Vaccines, ANCOVA, OLS Regression

1. Introduction

On December 8th, 2019, the first case of pneumonia disease caused by an unknown virus emerged in Wuhan City, Hubei Province, China. Virological investigation proved that this virus is a single-stranded RNA and it shares a lot of similarity with two others: the Middle East Respiratory Syndrome (henceforth, MERS) viral respiratory infection, also known as camel flu, caused by the MERS-coronavirus (henceforth, MERS-CoV), and the Severe Acute Respiratory Syndrome (henceforth, SARS) as a viral respiratory disease of zoonotic origin caused by SARS-coronavirus (henceforth, SARS-CoV or SARS-CoV-1). That's why, on February 11th, 2020, the World Health Organization (henceforth, WHO) officially named this virus as Coronavirus 2019, also called COVID-19. This disease spread rapidly around the world; thus, we counted until June 2020 more than 210 infected countries, more than 25,664,000 infected persons, and over 855,374 deaths. Obviously, our world is undergoing one of the most severe global health emergencies due to the COVID-19 virus.

Since COVID-19 vaccine is not currently available, Governments have imposed new precautionary measures in order to limit and slow the spread of this pandemic such as social distancing and quarantining. These measures are still insufficient and additional restrictions should be developed. In this context, with adopting another more scientific axis to overcome this disease, many researchers have started to decipher relations between existing vaccines and COVID-19 infection rate.

Indeed, a major debate has recently emerged concerning the impact of Bacillus Calmette–Guérin (BCG) vaccination on the transmission of COVID-19. Although they are not conclusive and decisive, some works (e.g., Gupta, 2020; Gursel and Gursel, 2020; Redelman-Sidi, 2020; Schaaf *et al.*, 2020) tried to identify whether BCG vaccination might have impacted the spread of COVID-19. For his part, Bouhamed (2020) succeeded to develop a prediction model that controlled the evolution of infected and recovered cases using a Deep Learning sequence prediction model and involving four possibilities according to the existence of BCG vaccination in the country and the Tuberculosis (TB) incidence per 100,000 individuals. His result concluded that the suspicions on the BCG vaccination and TB infections rates' implications turned out to be quite relevant.

It is in this framework that our work fits. In fact, the ultimate goal of this study is to clarify the links between existing vaccination and COVID-19. In other words, we seek to identify whether existing vaccination does confer natural protection and participate to limit COVID-19 spread. To achieve our goal, we apply sophisticated data and analysis including two econometric techniques, namely Analysis of Covariance (ANCOVA) and Ordinary Least Squares (OLS).

The remainder of this chapter is structured as follows: Section 2 describes the case of BCG vaccination, Section 3 provides a detailed description of the data used in this study, Section 4 presents the methodological framework and reports the empirical results, and finally Section 5 concludes the chapter.

2. BCG Vaccination

Miller *et al.* (1984) found that countries without universal policies of BCG vaccination (like the cases of Italy and USA) have been more severely affected compared to countries with universal BCG policies. They proposed that BCG vaccination could be attributed the reduced morbidity and mortality in countries with universal BCG policies.

In the same line, several studies have shown protective action of BCG against unrelated respiratory infections both in children and adults. A comparable protection effect of BCG on respiratory infections was shown among the elderly population in Indonesia

(Rosenberg *et al.*, 2020). Prospective clinical trial performed in Japan has shown BCG vaccine to protect from pneumonia in tuberculin-negative elderly populations (Gao *et al.*, 2020). Randomized controlled trials have demonstrated that the BCG vaccine has immunomodulatory effects to protect partially against respiratory infections. In South Africa, BCG-Danish reduced respiratory tract infections by 73% (95% CI, 39 to 88) in adolescents (Curtis *et al.*, 2020). Ozdemir *et al.* (2020) have shown proportionately less cases, milder illness, and a lower death rate in BCG vaccinated population as compared to BCG non-vaccinated across countries and hemispheres. According to Madan *et al.* (2020), BCG vaccination might alter a secondary innate immune response upon viral infection over a month apart resulting in improved antiviral responses and lowering viremia. Thus, it is so far proven that the countries more prone to be severely affected by SARS-CoV-2 did not adopt universal policies of BCG vaccination, like Italy and Spain. A reasonable explanation is that children of the country where routine childhood BCG vaccination is a policy and BCG vaccinated children have some degree of protection from infection from SARS-CoV-2 as well as less severe diseases among those who had been infected.

On the contrary, in particular work, Hamiel *et al.* (2020) studied the current policy of the Israeli Ministry of Health that tested for SARS-CoV-2 in every patient with symptoms that could be compatible with COVID-19 (cough, dyspnea, fever, etc.). Empirically, Chi-Square (χ^2) tests were used to compare proportions and rates per 100,000 population of positive test results among persons with symptoms compatible with COVID-19 born from 1979 to 1981 (aged 39–41 years) with those born from 1983 to 1985 (aged 35–37 years). A two-sided significance threshold was set at P-value less than 0.05 (typically $P \leq 0.05$). Of 72,060 test results reviewed, 3,064 were from patients born between 1979 and 1981 and 2,869 were among likely unvaccinated people born between 1983 and 1985. There was no statistically significant difference in the proportion of positive test results in the BCG-vaccinated group (361 [11.7%]) versus the unvaccinated group (299 [10.4%]; difference, 1.3%; 95% confidence interval [CI], -0.3% to 2.9%; $P = 0.09$) or in positivity rates per 100,000 (121 in vaccinated group versus 100 in unvaccinated group; difference, 21 per 100,000; 95% CI, -10 to 50 per 100,000; $P = 0.15$). There was one case of severe disease (mechanical ventilation or intensive care unit admission) in each group, and no deaths were reported. This study does not support the idea that BCG vaccination in childhood has a protective effect against COVID-19 in adulthood.

In the same line, the WHO (2020) affirmed that there is no evidence that BCG protects people against infection with the COVID-19 virus. Several studies have compared the incidence of COVID-19 in countries where the BCG vaccine is used and have observed that reported cases of COVID-19 were lower in countries where the new infants are systematically vaccinated against TB. According to the Belgian medical news site,[1,2] the BCG vaccine does not protect directly from COVID-19 but could provide a boost to the immune system. However, other factors must be taken into account such as the difference between national demographics, the morbidity rate, the COVID-19 screening rate, and the stage of the pandemic in each country, in order to specify that these studies were published in preprint, that is to say without peer validation (Ministry of Health, Labour, and Welfare of Japan, 2020).

3.   Data

Our chapter adds to the existing literature in different ways. The first contribution stems from the fact that we compile a huge database encompassing an important number of indicators covering 175 countries (see Appendix). All data are obtained from the World Bank and the WHO Websites. Indeed, we consider a set of 35 variables as follows:

1st Type: Dependent variable
Number of deaths per 100 infections (**ND**): this variable represents the evolution of deaths due to COVID-19 infections for 175 countries from the disease onset in each country until June 6, 2020.

---

[1]WHO (2020). Immunization in the context of COVID-19 pandemic. Frequently Asked Questions (FAQ). April 16, 2020. Available at: https://apps.who.int/iris/bitstream/handle/10665/331818/WHO-2019-nCoV-immunization_services-FAQ-2020.

[2]WHO (2020). BCG vaccination and COVID-19. Scientific Brief. April 12, 2020. Available at: https://www.who.int/news-room/commentaries/detail/bacille-calmette-gu%C3%A9rin-(bcg)-vaccination-and-covid-19.

2nd Type: *Quantitative variables*
— Percent of Population more than 65 years (**Pop**) as a demographic indicator: it turns out that *individuals who are elderly* register the *highest* death risk from *COVID*-19.

	Qualitative Independent Variables (Vaccines)	Abbreviation
1	Bacillus Calmette–Guérin	BCG
2	Diphtheria and Tetanus	DT
3	Diphtheria, Tetanus, Pertussis	DTaP
4	Diphtheria and Tetanus toxoids and whole-cell Pertussis	DTwP
5	Diphtheria, Tetanus, Pertussis, Hepatitis B, Polio, and Haemophilus influenza type b (DTaP-HB-IPV-Hib)	DTHIHB
6	Diphtheria and Tetanus Toxoid with Pertussis, Hib and HepB (DTwPHibHepB)	DTTPHHP
7	Hepatitis A for Adult (HepA_Adult)	HepA1
8	Hepatitis A for Child (HepA_Pediatric)	HepA2
9	Hepatitis B for Adult (HepB_Adult)	HepB1
10	Hepatitis B for Child (HepB_Pediatric)	HepB2
11	Haemophilus influenza type b	Hib
12	Human papillomavirus	HPV
13	Influenza Vaccine (Flu Vaccine)-Adult	IV1
14	Influenza Vaccine (Flu Vaccine)-Pediatric	IV2
15	Inactivated Polio Vaccine	IPV
16	Measles	Measles
17	Meningococcal ACY and W-135 diphtheria conjugate (MenACWY-135 conj)	MenACWY135
18	Meningococcal A conjugate (MenA_conj)	MenA
19	Meningococcal C conjugate (MenC_conj)	MenC
20	Measles, Mumps, and Rubella	MMR
21	Measles, Mumps, Rubella, and Varicella	MMRV
22	Measles-Rubella	MR
23	Oral Polio Vaccine	OPV
24	Pneumococcal Conjugate Vaccine	PCV
25	Pneumoccocal Polysacharide Vaccine (Pneumo_Ps)	PPV
26	Rotavirus	Rotavirus
27	Tetanus-Diphtheria	TD
28	Tetanus, Diphtheria, Pertussis	Tdap
29	Tetanus Toxoid	TT
30	Vitamin A	VitaminA
31	Yellow Fever	YF
32	Varicella-Zoster	VZ

— Crude death rate per 1,000 in 2018 (*CDR*) as a medical indicator: this variable is used to approximate the general health status by countries. In fact, due to a lack of data, we cannot collect a database concerning the mortality number per type of disease by country. In fact, many researchers prove that individuals with chronic health problems have a higher risk of mortality due to the COVID-19 infection.

3rd Type: Qualitative variables representing medical indicators, especially vaccination

These variables are binary. They take 1 if the vaccine is available in the country under consideration and 0 if not.

4. Methods and Results

Our empirical analysis is used to answer the following question: *Could an existing vaccination adopted by the different countries influence the number of deaths due to COVID-19?*

In other words, we are looking for the existence of significant links between vaccination and COVID-19 deaths. To reach our objective, we adopt two techniques: ANCOVA and OLS. A vaccine is considered as a powerful vector to control COVID-19 mortality if it is judged significant by the two techniques mentioned above.

To our best knowledge, there is hardly any research been done about the evolution of number of deaths per 100 COVID-19 infections involving this huge number of variables and countries and using these techniques.

In the rest of this part of our work, we apply a bottom-up scheme starting with the general data analysis to subsequently arrive at a more sophisticated and precise econometric analysis.

4.1. Covariance analysis (ANCOVA)

ANCOVA is a general linear model which combines Analysis of variance (ANOVA) and regression. It is considered among the most suitable techniques in presence of a quantitative endogenous variable and mixed (qualitative and quantitative) exogenous ones. More precisely, it is used to examine if the mean values of the dependent variables are equal across levels of categorical exogenous variables, while taking into account the influence of other continuous independent factors, known as covariates. Mathematically, ANCOVA decomposes the variance of the dependent variable into three main parts: variance explained by qualitative independent variables, variance explained by covariates, and residual variance. The general model of the analysis of covariance is formulated as follows:

$$Y_{ij} = \mu + \alpha_i + \beta(X_{ij} - \bar{X}_i) + \varepsilon_{ij} \tag{1}$$

where

- i is the category index of the categorical variable and j is the index of observations in each category;
- Y_{ij} is the *jth* observation under the *ith* categorical group for the dependent variable;
- X_{ij} represents the *jth* observation of the covariate under the *ith* group;
- μ is the general mean;
- α_i denotes the difference between the average of group i and the general average;
- β is the slope of the regression of the dependent variable on the quantitative independent variable;
- $\bar{X}_i$ is the mean of the quantitative independent variable for category i;
- ε_{ij} denotes the error term.

The premises of ANCOVA are also borrowed from those of ANOVA and linear regression:

- The relationship between the endogenous variable and the exogenous variables must be linear.
- The slope of this relation must be equal for the different modalities of the variable.
- The residues are independent and normally distributed.
- The residuals variance is homogeneous for the different modalities of the independent variable.

The estimation of Eq. (1) using ANCOVA method is summarized in Table 1.

Table 1: ANCOVA estimation results (Number of death, ND as a dependent variable).

Variables	Significance Test	Variables	Significance Test
Corrected Model	**.016****	IPV	.452
Intercept	**.046****	Measles	.228
Pop	.357	MenACWY135	.574
CDR	.452	MenA	.178
BCG	.502	MenC	**.057*****
DT	.284	MMR	.920
DtaP	.980	MMRV	.285
DTwP	.750	MR	.826
DTHIHB	.699	OPV	.444
DTTPHHB	.682	PCV	.719
HepA1	.637	PPV	.278
HepA2	.962	Rotavirus	.403
HepB1	**.033****	TD	**.096*****
HepB2	.594	Tdap	.569
Hib	.180	TT	.590
HPV	.308	VitaminA	.824
IV1	.653	YF	.929
IV2	.633	Varicella	**.095*****

Note: ** and *** indicate the significance at the thresholds of 5 and 10%, respectively.

Contrary to the doubts advanced in the existing literature, ANCOVA approach proves that BCG vaccination has no effect on COVID-19 mortality. Contrariwise, Hepatitis B-Adult (HepB1), MenC-conjugate (MenC), Tetanus-Diphtheria for older children/adults Vac-Cube (TD), and Varicella vaccination seems to be significant since their P-values are under the statistical level of 5 and 10%. Moreover, the model is globally significant since the P-value of the corrected model does not exceed the threshold of 5%. To be effective, the vaccine chosen must be immunogenic and well preserved between the subspecies of the target pathogen, in order to confer sufficient immunity.

In order to complete this analysis, we proceed to estimate the Number of deaths per 100 (ND) COVID-19 infections by adopting the OLS approach. This analysis is essential in order to ensure the significance of the variables highlighted by the ANCOVA approach as well as to determine the direction and height of the response following the stimulation of an explanatory variable.

4.2. OLS regression

In statistics, OLS regression is the most common estimation method and widely used to estimate the relationship between one or more exogenous qualitative or quantitative variables and the endogenous quantitative one as explained by the following formula:

$$y_i = \alpha + \beta_1 x_1 + \beta_2 x_2 + \cdots + \beta_n x_n + \varepsilon_i \tag{2}$$

where ε_i is an error term, α represents the constant term, and β_i represents the direct elasticities with respect to the different independent variables.

This method relies on the minimization of the sum of the squares in the difference between observed and estimated values of the endogenous variables.

Although it is used especially in the field of consumption analysis, our work is the only one that proposes OLS regression to inspect COVID-19 mortality. In fact, we will analyze in our chapter the following model:

$$\begin{aligned} \text{ND}_i = {} & \alpha + \beta_1 \text{Pop}_i + \beta_2 \text{CDR}_i + \beta_3 \text{BCG}_i + \beta_4 \text{DT}_i + \beta_5 \text{DTaP}_i \\ & + \beta_6 \text{DTwP}_i + \beta_7 \text{DTHIHB}_i + \beta_8 \text{DTTPHHB}_i + \beta_9 \text{HepA1}_i \\ & + \beta_{10} \text{HepA2}_i + \beta_{11} \text{HepB1}_i + \beta_{12} \text{HepB2}_i + \beta_{13} \text{HIB}_i + \beta_{14} \text{HPV}_i \\ & + \beta_{15} \text{IV1}_i + \beta_{16} \text{IV2}_i + \beta_{17} \text{IPV}_i + \beta_{18} \text{Measles}_i \\ & + \beta_{19} \text{MenACWY135}_i + \beta_{20} \text{MenA}_i + \beta_{21} \text{MenC}_i \\ & + \beta_{22} \text{MMR}_i + \beta_{23} \text{MMRV}_i + \beta_{24} \text{MR}_i + \beta_{25} \text{OPV}_i \\ & + \beta_{26} \text{PCV}_i + \beta_{27} \text{PPV}_i + \beta_{28} \text{Rotavirus}_i + \beta_{29} \text{TD}_i \\ & + \beta_{30} \text{Tdap}_i + \beta_{31} \text{TT}_i + \beta_{32} \text{VitaminA}_i + \beta_{33} \text{YF}_i \\ & + \beta_{34} \text{Varicella}_i + \varepsilon_i \end{aligned} \tag{3}$$

where i indicates the different countries under consideration in our empirical investigation.

Results of OLS regression are represented in Table 2. Evidently, OLS regression estimation has just confirmed results obtained using ANCOVA method. Indeed, our analysis uncovers three stylized facts.

Table 2: OLS estimation results (Number of deaths, ND, as a dependent variable).

Variables	Coef.	p-value	Variables	Coef.	p-value
Intercept	1.933	.812	IPV	−.696	.452
			Measles	1.259	.228
Pop	.096	.357	MenACWY135	.779	.574
CDR	.121	.452	MenA	−2.302	.178
BCG	.693	.502	MenC	**−2.500**	**.057*****
DT	.859	.284	MMR	−.120	.920
DtaP	.022	.980	MMRV	1.733	.285
DTwP	−.271	.750	MR	.207	.826
DTHIHB	.420	.699	OPV	.931	.444
DTTPHHB	.568	.682	PCV	.284	.719
HepA1	−.830	.637	PPV	1.102	.278
HepA2	.056	.962	Rotavirus	−.595	.403
HepB1	**−2.276**	**.033****	TD	**1.313**	**.096*****
HepB2	.385	.594	Tdap	−.525	.569
Hib	1.233	.180	TT	.432	.590
HPV	.720	.308	VitaminA	−.169	.824
IV1	−.704	.653	YF	−.078	.929
IV2	.694	.633	Varicella	**−1.568**	**.095*****

Note: ** and *** indicate the significance at the thresholds of 5, and 10%, respectively.

First, our investigation refutes the doubts of the protection provided by BCG vaccination against the mortality caused by COVID-19 infection. Second, OLS regression proves that three vaccines have a significant negative impact on the mortality number caused by COVID-19 disease. In fact, the P-value of HepB1 variable is under the statistical thresholds of 5% confirming, thus, that the number of deaths per 100 COVID-19 infections decreases by 2.276% for countries adopting Hepatitis B-Adult vaccine. This means that this vaccine is an inert peptide vaccine, which consists of only one or more proteins of the pathogen. However, in order to be effective, the peptides chosen must be immunogenic and well preserved between the subspecies of the target pathogen, in order to confer sufficient immunity (Alleman *et al.*, 2018).

Similarly, MenC and Varicella variables are statistically significant at the 10% level proving that COVID-19 mortality decline, respectively, by 2.5% and 1.568% for countries providing MenC-conjugate and Varicella vaccines to their citizens. In addition, we can also suggest that Varicella vaccination is an attenuated live vaccine essentially produced from attenuated viral strains by successive passages in culture on cells competent for viral replication. Since these vaccine strains are replicative, they perfectly mimic infection by the pathogenic germ in the vaccinated subject, which gives them excellent immunogenicity, in particular by activating innate immunity and CD8+ T lymphocytes and by inducing a prolonged memory response (Paul and Lelièvre, 2018). From this analysis, we can conclude that Hepatitis B adult, MenC-conjugate, and Varicella vaccination can boost immune system against COVID-19 infections. Another explanation to this result lies in the fact that the use of these vaccines can intervene to avoid the infection by chronic and severe diseases and subsequently complicate the situation more in case of COVID-19 infection.

Finally, contrary to our suspicions, it seems that Tetanus-Diphtheria (TD) vaccine has a positive and significant impact on mortality number due to COVID-19 disease at the 10% statistical level, with an increase of 1.313%.

In general, these vaccines are not very immunogenic because, by being reduced to only protective antigenic epitopes, they do not contain an agent able to amplify and orient innate immune responses then be adaptive. They require therefore the addition of adjuvants to be effective. They require also regular booster injections because they induce a short-lived memory response. However, the counterpart of this lack of efficiency is increased job security, with unrestricted use in immunocompromised subjects and very few side effects (Goullé and Grangeot-Keros, 2020).

4.3. Other factors

Some other factors are considered is this study, such as: (i) the number of days from diagnosis of the first patient with COVID-19 infection in each prefecture up to March 29, 2020; (ii) the populations that migrated to and from each prefecture in 2018 and which obtained from the annual report on internal migration in Japan derived from the basic resident registration; (iii) Inhabitable area that is calculated using data of the Statistics Bureau, Ministry of Internal Affairs and Communications; and (iv) the ratio of day to nighttime population, the ratio of households of five individuals or more to entire households, and the ratio of workers in the primary, secondary, and tertiary sectors of industry to the entire working population that was obtained from results of the national Census in 2015.

5. Conclusion

In this study, by applying ANCOVA and OLS regression on 35 variables and 175 countries, we tried to highlight the main vectors, especially among existing vaccinations, that influence the number of deaths due to COVID-19 infections. Evidently, we register a consensus between the two techniques about the role that Hepatitis B for Adult, MenC-conjugate, Varicella vaccine play in the reduction of COVID-19 mortality.

Contrary to our doubts, we reject the underlining hypothesis that BCG vaccine can be protective against COVID-19 mortality since only two techniques confirm it. This result does not invalidate that BCG vaccine might have impacted the transmission of COVID-19 infections. In addition, these vaccines are more purveyors of side effects than the others, and can in particular induce vaccine pathologies similar to the pathology against which they are supposed to protect in immunocompromised subjects (secondarily or constitutive). They are therefore formally contraindicated in these patients, as well as, as a precaution, in pregnant women (Alleman *et al.*, 2018).

So the side effects drastically and scientifically documented remain exceptional. The benefit–risk ratio is in favor of vaccines, and these have shown their effectiveness in reducing or even eradicating the transmission of pathogens associated with major morbidity and mortality. The emergence of new pathogens, and understanding the mechanisms of resistance to certain infectious agents, such as COVID-19, make it necessary to develop new vaccines and new adjuvants, but also new types of vaccines (DNA vaccines, viral pseudo-particles, viral vectors, . . .) which could allow new modes of activation of the immune system.

The findings arising from this analysis could help public health professionals and decision-makers to take the right decisions and procedures in order to stand up to this pandemic.

References

Alleman, M. M., Chitale, R., Burns, C. C. *et al.* (2018). Vaccine-derived poliovirus outbreaks and events — three provinces, Democratic Republic of the Congo, 2017. *Morbidity and Mortality Weekly Report,* **67**, pp. 300–305.

Bouhamed, H. (2020). COVID-19, Bacille Calmette–Guérin (BCG) and Tuberculosis: Cases and recovery previsions with deep learning sequence prediction. *Ingénierie des Systèmes d'Information,* **25**(2), pp. 165–172.

Curtis, N., Sparrow, A., Ghebreyesus, T. A. and Netea, M. G. (2020). Considering BCG vaccination to reduce the impact of COVID-19. *Lancet,* **395**(10236), pp. 1545–1546.

Gao, J., Tian, Z. and Yang, X. (2020). Breakthrough: Chloroquine phosphate has shown apparent efficacy in treatment of COVID-19 associated pneumonia in clinical studies. *BioScience Trends,* **14**(1), pp. 72–73.

Goullé, J. P. and Grangeot-Keros, L. (2020). Aluminum and vaccines: Current state of knowledge. *Médecine et Maladies Infectieuses,* **50**(1), pp. 16–21.

Gupta, A. (2020). Is immuno-modulation the key to COVID-19 pandemic? *Indian Journal of Orthopaedics,* **54**, pp. 394–397.

Gursel, M. and Gursel, I. (2020). Is global BCG vaccination-induced trained immunity relevant to the progression of SARS-CoV-2 pandemic? *Allergy,* **75**(7), pp. 1815–1819.

Hamiel, U., Kozer, E. and Youngster, I. (2020). SARS-CoV-2 rates in BCG-vaccinated and unvaccinated young adults. *JAMA,* **323**(22), pp. 2340–2341.

Madan, M., Pahuja, S., Mohan, A. *et al.* (2020). TB infection and BCG vaccination: are we protected from COVID-19? *Public Health,* **185**, pp. 91–92.

Miller, C. L., Morris, J. and Pollock, T. M. (1984). PHLS inquiry into current BCG vaccination policy. *British Medical Journal (Clinical Research Edition),* **288**(6416), p. 564.

Ministry of Health, Labour and Welfare of Japan. (2020). About Coronavirus Disease 2019 (COVID-19). https://www.mhlw.go.jp/stf/seisa kunitsuite/bunya/0000164708_00001.html.

Ozdemir, C., Kucuksezer, U. C. and Tamay, Z. U. (2020). Is BCG vaccination affecting the spread and severity of COVID-19? *Allergy,* **75**(7), pp. 1824–1827.

Paul, S. and Lelièvre, J. D. (2018). Immunologie fondamentale et immunopathologie. In: *Le mécanisme d'action des vaccins, le rôle des adjuvants*, Eds. Collège des enseignants d'immunologie, 2nd ed., Paris: Elsevier Masson, pp. 255–262.

Redelman-Sidi, G. (2020). Could BCG be used to protect against COVID-19? *Nature Reviews Urology*, **17**(6), pp. 316–317.

Rosenberg, E. S., Dufort, E. M., Udo, T. *et al.* (2020). Association of treatment with hydroxychloroquine or azithromycin with in-hospital mortality in patients with COVID-19 in New York State. *JAMA*, **323**(24), pp. 2493–2502.

Schaaf, H. S., du Preez, K., Kruger, M. *et al.* (2020). Bacille Calmette–Guérin (BCG) vaccine and the COVID-19 pandemic: Responsible stewardship is needed. *The International Journal of Tuberculosis and Lung Disease*, **24**(7), pp. 732–734.

WHO. (2020). Joining forces to end TB and COVID-19. https://www.who .int/news/item/12-05-2020-joining-forces-to-end-tb-and-covid-19.

Appendix

Afghanistan	Bulgaria	Equatorial Guinea	Iraq	Mauritania	Philippines	Sri Lanka
Albania	Burkina Faso	Eritrea	Iran	Mauritius	Poland	Sudan
Algeria	Burundi	Estonia	Ireland	Mexico	Portugal	Suriname
Andorra	Cabo Verde	Eswatini	Italy	Moldova Rep.	Qatar	Sweden
Angola	Cambodia	Ethiopia	Ivory Coast	Monaco	Romania	Switzerland
Antigua and Barbuda	Cameroon	Fiji	Jamaica	Mongolia	Russia	Syria
Argentina	Canada	Finland	Japan	Montenegro	Rwanda	Tajikistan
Armenia	Chad	France	Jordan	Morocco	Saint Lucia	Tanzania
Australia	Chile	Gabon	Kazakhstan	Mozambique	Saint Vincent and Grenadines	Thailand
Austria	China	Gambia	Kenya	Myanmar	Salvador	Timor-Leste
Azerbaijan	Colombia	Georgia	Kuwait	Namibia	San Marino	Togo
Bahamas	Comoros	Germany	Kyrgyzstan	Nepal	Sao Tome and Principe	Trinidad and Tobago Tobago
Bahrain	Congo	Ghana	Latvia	Netherlands	Saudi Arabia	Tunisia
Bangladesh	Costa Rica	Greece	Lebanon	New Zealand	Senegal	Turkey
Barbados	Croatia	Grenada	Lesotho	Nicaragua	Serbia	Uganda
Belarus	Cuba	Guatemala	Liberia	Niger	Seychelles	UK
Belgium	Cyprus	Guinea	Libya	Nigeria	Sierra Leone	Ukraine
Belize	Czech Rep.	Guinea-Bissau	Lithuania	North Macedonia	Singapore	Uruguay
Benin	Denmark	Guyana	Luxembourg	Norway	Slovakia	USA
Bhutan	Djibouti	Haiti	Madagascar	Oman	Slovenia	Uzbekistan
Bolivia	Dominica	Honduras	Malawi	Pakistan	Somalia	Venezuela
Bosnia and Herzegovina	Dominican Rep.	Hungary	Malaysia	Panama	South Africa	Vietnam
Botswana	Ecuador	Iceland	Maldives	Papua New Guinea	South Korea	Yemen
Brazil	Egypt	India	Mali	Paraguay	South Sudan	Zambia
Brunei Darussalam	Emirate	Indonesia	Malta	Peru	Spain	Zimbabwe

Chapter 2

Drivers of CO_2 Emissions in the Aftermath of the COVID-19 Pandemic

Soumaya Ben Khelifa* and **Sonia Arsi**[†]

Carthage Business School, University of Tunis Carthage, Tunis, Tunisia
* soumaya.benkhelifa@utctunisie.com
† sonia.arsi@utctunisie.com

The COVID-19 pandemic raised global warming issues, and particularly the effect of the carbon dioxide (CO_2) emissions. This is a matter of great concern especially in the aftermath of the forced confinement period, that reorganized the dices. Within this context, this chapter handles the relationship between CO_2 emissions, crude oil, and natural gas prices in the time of the critical epidemic. The results show that any decline in the natural gas and lagged crude oil prices downgrades carbon emissions. Equally, as the number of infected people by the disease increases, these emissions tend to decrease. This chapter provides implications for policymakers and governments.

Keywords: COVID-19, Carbon Emissions, Natural Gas, Crude Oil

1. Introduction

The global warming and climate change matters have become a topic of public debate. NASA Global Climate Change (2020) underlined that it tends to occur when "certain gases in the atmosphere block heat from escaping", which keeps the Earth warm; this is called

17

the "greenhouse effect". The main causes consist of carbon dioxide (CO_2) emissions and other gas polluters, like methane, nitrous oxide, chlorofluorocarbons, among others. In the year 2000, Robinson and Yamal (2000) reported that carbon emissions represent 72% of the annual gas emissions responsible for warming, followed by methane (18%) and nitrous oxide (9%). Interestingly, Global Carbon Project (2019) reported in the 2019 Carbon Budget that carbon emissions are projected to increase by 0.6% in 2019. Peters *et al.* (2020) added that this is a slow growth compared to previous years.

However, the world has been profoundly shaken by the COVID-19 pandemic and the effect has been even pointed out at the level of carbon emissions. In a recently released report, World Meterological Organization (2020) mentioned the forecasts on Global Carbon Project and reported that "CO_2 emissions in 2020 will fall by an estimated 4% to 7% due to COVID-19 confinement policies". The COVID-19 period is an attention-grabbing setting, as it reshaped equally the economic parameters. As denoted by Norouzi *et al.* (2020), the COVID-19 engendered a sharp change in the oil and electricity demand in China, considered among the drivers of carbon emissions (Global Carbon Project, 2019; Peters *et al.*, 2020). Besides, Rugani and Caro (2020) underlined the environmental effects of the COVID-19 in Italy. Particularly, Zhang *et al.* (2020) showed that forced lockdown during the pandemic decreased the level of pollution all around the world and induced better air quality.

In order to provide a boarder view of the times of the critical pandemic, this study aims to examine the relationship between carbon emissions, natural gas, and crude oil prices.

This chapter is organized as follows. Section 2 deals with the literature review on carbon emissions' drivers. Section 3 describes the data, followed by a depiction of the methodology in Section 4. The results are handled in Section 5. Finally, Section 6 concludes.

2.   Theoretical Background

As global warming is increasingly considered as a critical issue, the role of carbon emissions is significantly handled by researchers and academicians. The emerging strands of literature tend to focus on the diverse drivers of carbon emissions. This chapter emphasizes on the main research work.

Yang *et al.* (2020) tried to explain carbon emissions in China during the period 1996–2016. The results showed that coal is a significant factor pushing up the CO$_2$ emissions, followed by petroleum and natural gas at light percentages. On the same line, importing electricity contributes in reducing carbon emissions. Interestingly, the sectors' analysis pointed out that the industrial sector is a key force for carbon emissions. Malik *et al.* (2020) handled the carbon emissions' factors in Pakistan from 1971 to 2014. They found that foreign direct investments and economic growth lead to an upsurge of carbon emissions, this can be evidenced by the dominating part of the mining and quarrying sector. An intriguing result concerns any increase in oil prices, which tends to increase carbon emissions on the short-run, mainly due to subsidies that delayed energy consumption. However, the case is reverse in the long-run, as consumers are mainly looking for "energy-efficient" consumption. In the same way, Ullah *et al.* (2020) indicated that industrialization in Pakistan increased the CO$_2$ emissions, and the "consumption of energy-intensive goods and services" in turn over the period 1980–2018.

Besides, Lin and Li (2020) investigated the impact of electricity use across 114 countries from 2000 to 2014. It comes up that electricity use generated from clean energy contributes in degrading carbon emissions. Ehigiamusoe (2020) retained the same position regarding the electricity generated from renewable energy in 25 African countries from 1980–2016. The author added that electricity generated from oil, natural gas, and coal has a negative impact on CO$_2$ emissions. This can be mainly explained by the environmental features of each electricity source. The role of renewable energy in alleviating carbon emissions has been emphasized by researchers.

Cerdeira Bento and Moutinho (2016) indicated that CO$_2$ emissions reduced by an increase in the renewable electricity in Italy from 1990 to 2011. The same result was obtained by Dong *et al.* (2020) over the period 1995–2005 across 120 countries, Adedoyin *et al.* (2020) for the BRICS countries, and Dogan and Seker (2016) for the European Union.

Furthermore, Koçak *et al.* (2020) examined the impact of tourism on carbon emissions. The authors pointed out that countries recording a high number of tourists' arrival display an increase in carbon emissions for the period 1995–2014. A potential explanation relies on the extensive use by tourists of transportation services. In this context, Huang *et al.* (2019) underlined the positive effect of energy use technology on CO_2 transport emissions in China.

It is underlined that drivers, and especially energy factors, still have a significant impact on carbon emissions. However, they tend to differ depending on the context. Interestingly, the period of the COVID-19 pandemic showed a behavior change in the CO_2 emissions. Indeed, the recent work of Le Quéré *et al.* (2020) highlighted that CO_2 emissions decreased during the period of the lockdown. This was mainly due to the quasi-absence of overall activity around the world. In Italy, Rugani and Caro (2020) showed that carbon footprint decreased during the lockdown period compared to normal times, and this effect is mainly perceivable in the industrialized zones. Faced with the limited number of studies dealing with carbon emissions during the pandemic period, this chapter tries to fill in the gap and examines the potential energy drivers of carbon emissions during that phase.

3.   Data

The data used in this study includes daily observations of crude oil prices, COVID-19 measured as the number of infected people, natural gas prices, and carbon emissions. The study period of selected data is from January 6, 2020 to June 11, 2020, yielding 110 observations. All data series are transformed into natural logarithmic series. Table 1 describes data and sources.

Table 1:   Data elaboration and sources.

Variables	Description	Source
CO_2	Daily Carbon Emissions (Metric Tons CO_2 ($MTCO_2$) per day)	Integrated Carbon Observation System
Crude Oil	Daily Crude Oil WTI Spot Price (Dollar per Barrel)	U.S. Energy Information Administration
Natural Gas	Daily Natural Gas Price (U.S. Dollar)	www.investing.com
Infected People	Daily Cumulative Population Infected	World Health Organization (WHO)

4. Methodology

In this chapter, the ARDL (Autoregressive Distributed Lag) approach is performed to estimate the relationship between carbon emissions and energy (crude oil and natural gas prices) in the times of pandemic conditions. The ARDL model has been used by Norouzi *et al.* (2020) to investigate China' energy and electricity demand pattern during the COVID-19 crisis.

Based on Pesaran and Smith (1995) and Pesaran *et al.* (2001)'s ADRL methodology, we firstly use the ARDL bounds test for cointegration to examine whether there is a dynamic relationship between carbon emissions, crude oil, and natural gas prices during the critical epidemic. The suggested pattern is shown as follows:

$$\Delta \ln \text{CO}_{2_t} = \alpha_0 + \sum_{i=1}^{p} \alpha_1 \Delta \ln \text{CO}_{2_{t-i}} + \sum_{i=1}^{p} \alpha_2 \Delta \ln \text{Oil}_{t-i}$$

$$+ \sum_{i=1}^{p} \alpha_3 \Delta \ln \text{Gas}_{t-i} + \sum_{i=1}^{p} \alpha_4 \Delta \ln \text{Infected people}_{t-i}$$

$$+ \beta_1 \ln \text{CO}_{2_{t-1}} + \beta_2 \ln \text{Oil}_{t-1}$$

$$+ \beta_3 \ln \text{Gas}_{t-1} + \beta_4 \ln \text{Infected people}_{t-1} + \varepsilon_t \quad (1)$$

where $\Delta \ln \text{CO}_2$, $\Delta \ln \text{Oil}$, $\Delta \ln \text{Gas}$, and $\Delta \ln \text{Infected}$ people represent their respective difference values. α_1 to α_4 represent short-term dynamic relationships, while, β_1 to β_4 are related to the long-run dynamic relationship. P is the lag period of the dependent variable and each independent variable, respectively. The ARDL bounds test is based on the Wald or F-statistic for a joint significance test to verify if there is a cointegration relationship. Hence, the hypotheses are presented as follows:

H$_0$: $\beta_1 = \beta_2 = \beta_3 = \beta_4$: there is no cointegration relationship, if the estimated F-statistic is less than the lower bound of the boundary value.

H$_1$: $\beta_1 \neq \beta_2 \neq \beta_3 \neq \beta_4 \neq 0$: there is cointegration relationship, if the estimated F-statistic is more than the lower bound of the boundary value.

Secondly, we estimate the long and short-run results and perform diagnostic tests to verify model stability.

If there is no cointegration, we use the following ARDL model:

$$\Delta \ln CO_{2t} = \alpha_0 + \sum_{i=1}^{p} \alpha_1 \Delta \ln CO_{2t-i}$$

$$+ \sum_{i=1}^{p} \alpha_2 \Delta \ln Oil_{t-i} + \sum_{i=1}^{p} \alpha_3 \Delta \ln Gas_{t-i}$$

$$+ \sum_{i=1}^{p} \alpha_4 \Delta \ln Infected\ people_{t-i} + \varepsilon_t \qquad (2)$$

If there is cointegration, the ARDL-ECM model is presented as follows:

$$\Delta \ln CO_{2t} = \alpha_0 + \sum_{i=1}^{p} \alpha_1 \Delta \ln CO_{2t-i}$$

$$+ \sum_{i=1}^{p} \alpha_2 \Delta \ln Oil_{t-i} + \sum_{i=1}^{p} \alpha_3 \Delta \ln Gas_{t-i}$$

$$+ \sum_{i=1}^{p} \alpha_4 \Delta \ln Infected\ people_{t-i} + \theta ECT_{t-1} + \varepsilon_t \qquad (3)$$

where θ is the long-run equilibrium speed of adjustment parameter, and ECT represents the error correction term.

5.   Empirical Results

5.1.   Descriptive statistics

Table 1 reports descriptive statistics of the variables of the study. We observe wide dispersions and variations among variables. The average crude oil price, carbon emissions, natural gas price, and infected people were 35.864 U.S. dollars per barrel, 91.52882 MTCO$_2$/day, 1.824927 U.S. dollars, and 1,812,508, respectively. Their standard deviations were 16.39488, 5.079312, 0.1427744, and 2,252,738, respectively, indicating the wide spread of the data around the mean for crude oil prices, carbon emissions, and infected people. The COVID-19 pandemic adversely impacts crude oil prices. On April 20, 2020, the latter fell to its minimum value (−36.98), a level not seen since 2002. In fact, strict quarantine measures have been taken in

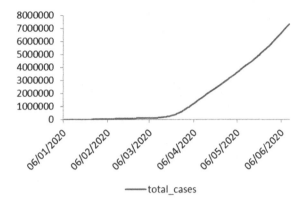

Figure 1:   Trends of the number of infected people.

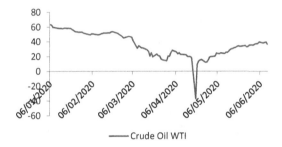

Figure 2:   Trends in crude oil WTI prices.

many countries to reduce the spread of COVID-19 pandemic. Hence, oil demand has dropped sharply, which led to downward pressure on prices.

Figure 1 shows that the number of infected people increased steeply during the study period. It was equal to 59 cases in January 6, 2020, and reached 7,322,385 infected people in June 11, 2020, representing an increase of 12,410,722% during the period. Figure 2 displays that the crude oil prices fell rapidly, reaching a historic slump by May 6, 2021. Figures 3 and 4 show that carbon emissions and natural gas prices recorded a downward trend, suggesting that the variables may have some associations.

5.2.   Unit root tests

We investigate the stationarity properties of the variables based on Augmented Dickey–Fuller (ADF) test. Table 2 provides the findings

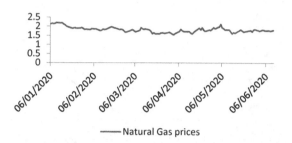

Figure 3:   Trends in natural gas prices.

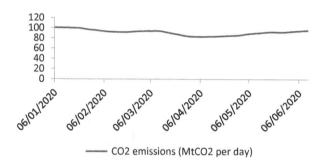

Figure 4:   Trends in carbon emissions.

Table 2:   Descriptive statistics.

Variable	N	Mean	Standard Deviation	Minimum	Maximum
Crude Oil	110	35.86445	16.39488	−36.98	63.27
Natural Gas	110	1.824927	0.1427744	1.552	2.202
Infected People	110	1812508	2252738	59	7322385
CO_2	110	91.52882	5.079312	83.04	100.24

of the unit root test in levels and first difference of the natural logarithms of the variables. The test shows that only natural gas prices and infected people are stationary at level. However, crude oil prices and carbon emissions are stationary at first difference. The null hypothesis of unit root is rejected for all variables used in the study, meaning that they are either integrated of order one or zero. Therefore, the ARDL procedure can be employed in this study.

5.3.   Lag length test

Lag lengths are very important for cointegration. We use different criteria to determine the appropriate optimum lag-length (LR, FPE, AIC, HQIC, and SBIC). Malik *et al.* (2020) also employ these five criteria to identify the suitable lag length. Table 3 reports the findings for lag order selection. All criteria (except SBIC) suggest a lag length of 2 for the cointegration. Finally, we construct the matrix list to identify the most suitable ARDL model. Table 4 presents the results. We find that ARDL (2, 2, 2, 1) is the most appropriate model (Table 5).

5.4.   Cointegration analyses (ARDL bounds test)

We check for cointegration through the ARDL bounds test provided by Pesaran *et al.* (2001). We analyze the Joint-F significance test for

Table 3:   Unit root test "ADF test".

Variable	t-statistic	p-value
Level		
Crude Oil	-1.588	0.4896
Natural Gas	$(-3.329)^{**}$	0.0136
Infected people	$(-3.325)^{**}$	0.0138
CO$_2$	-1.55	0.5088
First Difference		
Crude Oil	$(-7.509)^{***}$	0
Natural Gas	$(-8.554)^{***}$	0
Infected people	$(-5.555)^{***}$	0
CO$_2$	$(-3.083)^{**}$	0.0278

Note: ***, **indicate significance at 1 and 5 level, respectively.

Table 4:   Lag selection.

Lag	LR	FPE	AIC	HQIC	SBIC
0		3.00E–06	-1.37225	-1.33128	-1.27114
1	1315.9	1.50–E11	-13.6001	-13.3953	-13.0946^*
2	55.595^*	$1.2E–11^*$	-13.8248^*	-13.4561^*	-12.9149

Note: *indicates statistical significance at the critical level of 10%.

Table 5:   Matrix list e(lags).

	CO_2	Crude Oil	Natural Gas	Infected People
e(lags)[1,4]	2	2	2	1

Table 6:   ARDL bounds test.

H_0: no levels relationship

F-Bounds Test Statistics

F-statistic	3.351
t	−2.006

	I(0)	I(1)	I(0)	I(1)	I(0)	I(1)	I(0)	I(1)
	10%		5%		2.50%		1%	
k_3	2.72	3.77	3.23	4.35	3.69	4.89	4.29	5.61

Eq. (1) against the critical values proposed by Pesaran *et al.* (2001). The estimated F-statistic for the ARDL bounds test are shown in Table 6. The findings suggest that the value of the calculated F-statistic is below the lower bound of the critical value. Hence, we accept the null hypothesis of no cointegration, indicating the non-existence of a long-run relationship between the dependent variable carbon emissions and its set of covariates: crude oil price, natural gas price, and infected people. Malik *et al.* (2020) find evidence of a long-run association among the dependent variable carbon emissions and its explanatory variables oil price, FDI, and per capita income in Pakistan, during the period of 1971–2014.

5.5.   ARDL estimates

Since there is no cointegration among variables, the relationship between variables is modeled using Eq. (1). Table 7 summarizes the results of ARDL estimates. The findings for the relationship between carbon emissions and the current crude oil price is not statistically significant. However, the crude oil price lagged by one day is positively and significantly associated with carbon emissions, indicating that the substantial fall in oil prices decreases environmental degradation, during the COVID-19 pandemic. In fact, the epidemic severeness significantly impacts the petroleum demand Norouzi *et al.* (2020), which generates a fall in oil prices. Ehigiamusoe (2020) shows that electricity generation from oil is positively related to carbon emissions in African countries during the period 1980–2016.

Table 7:   ARDL estimates.

ARDL (2,2,2,1) Regression	
Dependent Variable	**CO$_2$**
Explanatory Variables	**Coefficient**
CO$_2$	
L1	1.390918***
	15.98
L2	(-0.4194197)***
	-4.93
Crude Oil	
–	-0.0027504
	-0.93
L1	0.0104298***
	2.77
L2	-0.004787
	-1.54
Natural Gas	
–	0.0230822**
	2.11
L1	-0.0152087
	-1.05
L2	0.0214072**
	2.01
Infected People	
–	(-0.0052711)***
	-2.95
L1	0.0058386***
	3.37
C	0.0945403
	1.62
N	107
R-squared	0.9957

Note: ** and *** indicate the significance at critical levels of 5% and 10%, respectively.

Table 8:   Diagnostic tests.

Durbin–Watson d-Statistic (11, 107) = 2.150273			
Breusch–Godfrey LM test for Autocorrelation			
lags(p)	chi^2	df	Prob > chi^2
1	1.834	1	0.1756

H_0: no serial correlation

White's Test for H_0: homoskedasticity
against H_a: unrestricted heteroskedasticity
chi^2(65) = 92.76
Prob > chi^2 = 0.0135
Cameron & Trivedi's Decomposition of IM-Test

Source	chi^2	df	p
Heteroskedasticity	92.76	65	0.0135
Skewness	6.8	10	0.7444
Kurtosis	1.77	1	0.1837
Total	101.32	76	0.0278

Then, the results show that natural gas price enters with a positive and significant coefficient, suggesting that natural gas price has deleterious impact on carbon emissions. Nevertheless, the natural gas price has recorded a downward trend, in the time of the critical epidemic. Hence, one U.S. dollar decrease in natural gas price will lessen carbon emissions by 0.023 MTCO$_2$/day during this period.

Finally, we find that the number of infected people has statistically negative and significant association with carbon emissions, during the COVID-19 pandemic. Indeed, if the number of infected people increases by one individual, carbon emissions will decrease by 0.0053 MTCO$_2$/day. This can be explained by the confinement required by many countries during this critical period, which contributes significantly in reducing the movement of citizens. Table 8 presents the diagnostic tests. The findings highlight that there is no serial correlation.

6.   Conclusion

Climate and carbon emissions have been a key issue during these recent years. Within this framework, this chapter examines the impact of crude oil and natural gas prices on CO$_2$ emissions during the COVID-19 pandemic period, specifically between January 6th and June 11th, 2020. The outcomes underline that any decrease in the crude oil lagged price and natural gas price induces a decline in carbon emissions. This is mainly due to the sharp decrease in energy consumption during this pandemic period. Whereas, there is a significant and negative impact of the number of infected people, indicating that carbon emissions' reduction is perceived as the number of COVID-19 infected individuals rises, which is explained by the forced lockdown.

This chapter provides diverse implications, as it leads policymakers to think about efficient solutions. Yang *et al.* (2020) underlined that extensive advance in terms of clean energy and "imported electricity" can help in decreasing carbon emissions. Equally, governments and financial institutions have to ease investments on renewable energy Malik *et al.* (2020). They should apply rigorous rules related to environmental protection.

The study is not without limitations. First, the study included only the first main wave of the COVID-19 pandemic period. Second, the factors impacting the carbon emissions were restricted to energy consumption, displayed by crude oil and natural gas.

Further research can overcome these shortcomings. It can extend the study period and include the second wave of COVID-19. Equally, a cross-country breakdown can be considered to cope with differences between countries. And, the incorporation of additional factors, like electricity consumption among others, can enrich the analysis and give handy inferences.

References

Adedoyin, F. F., Gumede, M. I., Bekun, F. V., Etokakpan, M. U., and Balsalobre-lorente, D. (2020). Modelling coal rent, economic growth and CO$_2$ emissions: Does regulatory quality matter in BRICS economies? *Science of the Total Environment*, **710**, DOI: 10.1016/j.scitotenv.2019.136284.

Cerdeira Bento, J. P. and Moutinho, V. (2016). CO$_2$ emissions, non-renewable and renewable electricity production, economic growth, and international trade in Italy. *Renewable and Sustainable Energy Reviews*, **55**, pp. 142–155.

Dogan, E. and Seker, F. (2016). Determinants of CO_2 emissions in the European Union: The role of renewable and non-renewable energy. *Renewable Energy*, **94**, pp. 429–439.

Dong, K., Dong, X., and Jiang, Q. (2020). How renewable energy consumption lower global CO_2 emissions? Evidence from countries with different income levels. *World Economy*, **43**(6), pp. 1665–1698.

Ehigiamusoe, K. U. (2020). A disaggregated approach to analyzing the effect of electricity on carbon emissions: Evidence from African countries. *Energy Reports*, **6**, pp. 1286–1296.

Global Carbon Project. (2019). 2019 Carbon Budget. https://www.global carbonproject.org/carbonbudget/19/presentation.htm.

Huang, F., Zhou, D., Wang, Q., and Hang, Y. (2019). Decomposition and attribution analysis of the transport sector's carbon dioxide intensity change in China. *Transportation Research Part A: Policy and Practice*, **119**, pp. 343–358.

Koçak, E., Ulucak, R., and Ulucak, Z. Ş. (2020). The impact of tourism developments on CO_2 emissions: An advanced panel data estimation. *Tourism Management Perspectives*, **33**, https://doi.org/10.1016/j.tmp.2019.100611.

Le Quéré, C., Jackson, R. B., Jones, M. W., Smith, A. J. P., Abernethy, S., Andrew, R. M., De-Gol, A. J., Willis, D. R., Shan, Y., Canadell, J. G., Friedlingstein, P., Creutzig, F., and Peters, G. P. (2020). Temporary reduction in daily global CO_2 emissions During the COVID-19 forced confinement. *Nature Climate Change*, **10**, pp. 647–653.

Lin, B. and Li, Z. (2020). Is more use of electricity leading to less carbon emission growth? An analysis with a panel threshold model. *Energy Policy*, **137**, https://doi.org/10.1016/j.enpol.2019.111121.

Malik, M. Y., Latif, K., Khan, Z., Butt, H. D., Hussain, M., and Nadeem, M. A. (2020). Symmetric and asymmetric impact of oil price, FDI and economic growth on carbon emission in Pakistan: Evidence from ARDL and non-linear ARDL approach. *Science of the Total Environment*, **726**, https://doi.org/10.1016/j.scitotenv.2020.138421.

NASA Global Climate Change. (2020). The Causes of Climate Change. https://climate.nasa.gov/causes/.

Norouzi, N., Zarazua de Rubens, G., Choubanpishehzafar, S., and Enevoldsen, P. (2020). When pandemics impact economies and climate change: Exploring the impacts of COVID-19 on oil and electricity demand in China. *Energy Research and Social Science*, **68**, https://doi.org/10.1016/j.erss.2020.101654.

Pesaran, M. H., Shin, Y., and Smith, R. J. (2001). Bounds testing approaches to the analysis of level relationships. *Journal of Applied Econometrics*, **16**, pp. 289–326.

Pesaran, M. H. and Smith, R. (1995). Estimating long-run relationships from dynamic heterogeneous panels. *Journal of Econometrics*, **68**, pp. 79–113.

Peters, G. P., Andrew, R. M., Canadell, J. G., Friedlingstein, P., Jackson, R. B., Korsbakken, J. I., Le Quéré, C., and Peregon, A. (2020). Carbon dioxide emissions continue to grow amidst slowly emerging climate policies. *Nature Climate Change*, **10**, pp. 3–6.

Robinson, B. and Yamal, B. (2000). Proximate causes of climate change: The human activities that cause climate change. https://www.e-education.psu.edu/geog438w/node/364.

Rugani, B. and Caro, D. (2020). Impact of COVID-19 outbreak measures of lockdown on the Italian carbon footprint. *Science of the Total Environment*, **737**, https://doi.org/10.1016/j.scitotenv.2020.139806.

Ullah, S., Ozturk, I., Usman, A., Majeed, M. T., and Akhtar, P. (2020). On the asymmetric effects of premature deindustrialization on CO₂ emissions: Evidence from Pakistan. *Environmental Science and Pollution Research*, **27**(30), pp. 13692–13702.

World Meterological Organization. (2020). United in Science Report 2020: Climate Change has not Stopped for COVID19. September. https://public.wmo.int/en/media/press-release/united-science-report-climate-change-has-not-stopped-covid19.

Yang, J., Cai, W., Ma, M., Li, L., Liu, C., Ma, X., Li, L., and Chen, X. (2020). Driving forces of China's CO₂ emissions from energy consumption based on Kaya-LMDI methods. *Science of the Total Environment*, **711**(April), DOI: 10.1016/j.scitotenv.2019.134569.

Zhang, Z., Arshad, A., Zhang, C., Hussain, S., and Li, W. (2020). Unprecedented temporary reduction in global air pollution associated with COVID-19 forced confinement: A continental and city scale analysis. *Remote Sensing*, **12**, p. 2420.

Chapter 3

Bitcoin and the First Wave of COVID-19

John W. Goodell[*,‡] and **Stéphane Goutte**[†,§]

University of Akron Department of Finance, Akron, Ohio, United States

†*Université Paris-Saclay, UVSQ, CEMOTEV, 78280 Guyancourt, France*

‡*johngoo@uakron.edu*

§*stephane.goutte@uvsq.fr*

Extending the time period of Goodell and Goutte (2020), we apply wavelet methods to daily data of COVID-19 world deaths and daily Bitcoin prices from December 31, 2019 to August 31, 2020. We confirm Goodell and Goutte (2020) for an extended period by evidencing a positive correlation between levels of COVID-19 and Bitcoin prices, suggesting Bitcoin as a safe haven investment. Investigations such as this are important to both scholars and policy-makers, as well as investment professionals interested in the financial implications of both COVID-19 and cryptocurrencies.

Keywords: Market Co-movement, COVID-19, Bitcoin, Cryptocurrencies

1. Introduction

As 2020 comes to a close, the COVID-19 pandemic is still ongoing, with in many regions of the globe unprecedented levels of cases and deaths. While the eventual scale of the disaster is not yet determined, the initial deployment of vaccinations suggests the possibility of the "end of the beginning". We are all now tragically familiar with the ongoing enormous costs in lives of this pandemic. However, we are also concerned about the eventual economic impact of this crisis, including the impact on financial markets. In response to this, a number of researchers have investigated the association of COVID-19 with the movement of cryptocurrencies.

We include ourselves in these efforts. In a recent article (Goodell and Goutte, 2020), we apply wavelet methodology (Grinsted *et al.*, 2004; Kang *et al.*, 2019) to daily data of COVID-19 world deaths and daily Bitcoin prices from December 31, 2019 to April 29, 2020, finding that levels of COVID-19 caused a rise in Bitcoin prices. This effect is especially strong for the portion of our period post April 5. The results of Goodell and Goutte (2020), as well as others, are particularly meaningful when considering that COVID-19 catalyzes greater concern for future economic costs, and likely greater economic uncertainty.

It is important to understand how the role of Bitcoin in hedging other assets has changed during the period of the COVID-19 crisis. Understandably, there are few studies yet on such recent events. An exception is Conlon and McGee (2020), who show that Bitcoin has indeed been a poor hedge against the SP500 during the COVID-19 crisis.

While Goodell and Goutte (2020) evidence Bitcoin as acting as a safe haven similar to gold, others, (e.g., Chen *et al.*, 2020; Conlon *et al.*, 2020; Conlon and McGee, 2020) find that COVID-19, perhaps because of general apprehension, has an adverse effect on Bitcoin returns, nullifying the role of Bitcoin as a safe haven asset. Additionally, others find that cryptocurrencies do not act as a hedge or safe haven during extreme financial and economic downturns (Conlon and McGee, 2020).

Certainly, the role of cryptocurrencies in investment portfolios, post COVID-19, will continue to be of interest. As noted by Goodell (2020) and others, COVID-19 will not only engender immediate ongoing economic costs, but likely change attitudes toward risk and investment that we will discover only in time.

As gold is often considered to move with economic policy uncertainty (Raza *et al.*, 2018), it is natural to extend this inquiry to cryptocurrencies. Certainly, there are numerous studies investigating the co-movement of Bitcoin and similar currencies with movement in global economic uncertainty. Again, this area is not settled.

For instance, Wu *et al.* (2019) and Wang *et al.* (2019) find a negligible relationship, while Bouri *et al.* (2018) and Demir *et al.* (2018) find a stronger relationship.

It is also reasonable to consider further the movement of Bitcoin with other assets, particularly in the context of changes in economic apprehension. After all, economic conditions manifest to financial markets through changes in asset prices. While Bouri *et al.* (2017b), Klein *et al.* (2018), and Smales (2019) do not find consistent evidence that Bitcoin serves as a safe haven for global assets, show that Bitcoin, like gold, serves as a hedge, safe haven, and diversifier for oil price movements. However, this property seems to be sensitive to Bitcoin's and gold's different (bear, normal, or bull) market conditions and to whether the oil price is in a downside, normal, or upside regime. Kurka (2019) finds that the relationship between Bitcoin and other assets depends on proximity to shocks. Further, Matkovskyy and Jalan (2019) find that, during crisis periods, risk-averse investors tend to move away from Bitcoin, with a view that it is riskier than financial markets. In these regards, Goutte *et al.* (2019) offer a comprehensive survey of cryptofinance and mechanisms of exchange.

In this chapter, we report results of updating Goodell and Goutte (2020) by extending the period of investigation through the end of August. While this investigation essentially confirms earlier studies, given the unprecedented, and therefore unknown, nature of COVID-19, we feel it is important to extend previous studies to see if results hold for several additional months beyond initial investigations. Overall, studies such as this, examining how Bitcoin prices co-move with the intensity of the COVID-19 crisis, contribute to our understanding of how Bitcoin might provide diversification benefits, or act as a hedge, or safe haven during extreme crises.

2. Data and Econometric Framework

This study applies the wavelet method of Grinsted *et al.* (2004) to daily data of COVID-19 world deaths and Bitcoin prices from December 31, 2019 to August 31, 2020. We employ the methodology stated in Goodell and Goutte (2020). We compute the daily returns by finding the difference between two consecutive prices:

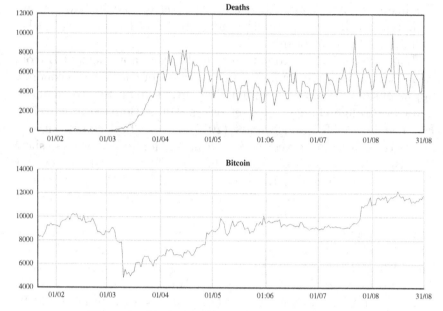

Figure 1:   Evolution dynamics of the return series.

Table 1:   Descriptive statistics.

	Covid Deaths	Bitcoin
Mean	3827.205	9113.400
Std. Deviation	2501.887	1619.568
Min	0	4927
Max	10132	12300
Skewness	1.272	−3.507
Kurtosis	2.045	2.88

$ri, t = P_{i,t-}P_{i,t-1}$ where i is for COVID-19 deaths and Bitcoin.
Figure 1 shows the dynamics of the return series and illustrates
the stylized factors (e.g., volatility clustering) for the Bitcoin return
series.

We see in Fig. 1 that the dynamic of the COVID-19 pandemic is a
two-phase process: an exponential increasing of the deaths' number
until middle of April, then a quite stable oscillating dynamic.

Table 1 presents descriptive statistics of the return series.

As shown in Table 1, Bitcoin exhibits skewing, as well as excess kurtosis. These findings and the Shapiro-Wilk statistics demonstrate that the distributions of this series is asymmetric and leptokurtic, rejecting the normality property. As the series are asymmetric and leptokurtic, we consider that wavelet analysis is the appropriate tool. Wavelet analysis, rather than assessing an average statistical relationship, investigates co-movement with time, as well as frequency.

2.1. Wavelet coherence

We apply continuous wavelet power spectrum and coherence methodologies between COVID-19 deaths and Bitcoin return prices. This is illustrated in Fig. 2. It illustrates the wavelet coherence and phase difference between COVID-19 deaths and Bitcoin return prices. We can identify several significant high-degree co-movements between COVID-19 deaths and Bitcoin.

- A one-month lag between the beginning of April and the middle of May.
- A one-week lag between the 10th of June and the 10th of July.

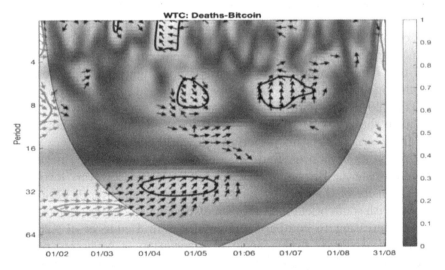

Figure 2: Wavelet coherency (WTC) between COVID-19 deaths and Bitcoin.

- A two-day frequency cycle observed during the period 8th March to 10th March and another one during the period 10th April to 30th April.
- A particularly meaningful and significant coherence for 5–8 day frequency cycles observed during the period of roughly the middle of April to the middle of May.

These coherences evidence a contagion effect mainly during the full global manifestation of COVID-19. Although results also confirm Goodell and Goutte (2020) regarding positive association of Bitcoin and levels of COVID during the earlier phase of the pandemics' impact on Western economies.

We also discern causality and phase differences between COVID-19 deaths and Bitcoin returns. Arrows indicate phase differences between COVID-19 deaths and Bitcoin returns. For example, and indicate that both COVID-19 deaths and Bitcoin returns are in-phase and out of phase. Being in-phase (out of phase) indicates a positive (negative) correlation between COVID-19 deaths and Bitcoin returns. Moreover, an upper right arrow and lower left arrow indicate that COVID-19 deaths are leading Bitcoin return prices, while a lower right arrow and upper left one indicates COVID-19 deaths' values are lagging those of Bitcoin return prices.

Consequently, as shown in Fig. 2, we can identify causality and phase differences between COVID-19 deaths and Bitcoin return prices. We observe that since 5th April, the main and most significant period of coherence and co-movements in both 1–2 days and 3–7-day bands, arrows are in majority upper right and right arrows, signifying an in-phase relationship and a positive correlation between COVID-19 deaths and Bitcoin returns. Moreover, these arrows also indicate that COVID-19 deaths led Bitcoin returns in the short and medium terms, over this period of full world containment.

In summary, we find predominantly a strong negative co-movement of Bitcoin prices and COVID-19. However, levels of the intensity of this co-movement do vary over our overall period of study, with some brief intervals even exhibiting a positive association. It is interesting to compare our results with Demir *et al.* (2018). Demir *et al.* (2018) find a negative association of economic policy uncertainty with Bitcoin only for extreme values of this uncertainty.

Certainly COVID-19 is an extreme event, with likely an extreme impact on peoples' perception of uncertainty. Our results may result in more questions than answers for future research. For instance, how does the co-movement of Bitcoin with COVID-19 compare with the co-movements of national financial markets with the pandemic? Why were there strong but brief periods of negative co-movement of Bitcoin with COVID-19 as early as February 10? Could Bitcoin have a signaling value? Many of these questions are outside the bounds of this chapter.

3. Conclusions

We apply wavelet methods to daily data of COVID-19 world deaths and daily Bitcoin prices from December 31, 2019 to August 31, 2020, evidencing that levels of COVID-19 cause a rise in Bitcoin prices. Extending the time period of Goodell and Goutte (2020), we apply wavelet methods to daily data of COVID-19 world deaths and daily Bitcoin prices. We confirm Goodell and Goutte (2020) for an extended period by evidencing a positive correlation between levels of COVID-19 and Bitcoin prices, suggesting Bitcoin as a safe haven investment. We find particularly strong positive relationships between Bitcoin and COVID-19 over a variety of segments in our time period, particularly from roughly the middle of April to the middle of May, and from the middle of June to the middle of July. We also confirm the results of Goodell and Goutte (2020) for the period in early March closer to the beginning of the COVID-19 downturn in western economies. As there is considerable academic interest in the hedging, diversifying, and safe-haven qualities of Bitcoin, investigations such as this are important to both scholars and policy-makers, as well as investment professionals interested in the financial implications of both COVID-19 and cryptocurrencies.

References

Bouri, Elie, Rangan Gupta, Chi K. M. Lau, David Roubaud, and Shixuan Wang (2018). Bitcoin and global financial stress: A copula-based approach to dependence and causality in the quantiles, *Quarterly Review of Economics and Finance*, **69**, pp. 297–307.

Conlon, Thomas and Richard J. McGee (2020). Safe haven or risky hazard? Bitcoin during the COVID-19 bear market, *Finance Research Letters*, Vol. 35. https://doi.org/10.1016/j.frl.2020.101607.

Conlon, Thomas, Shaen Corbet, and Richard J. McGee (2020). Are cryptocurrencies a safe haven for equity markets? An international perspective from the COVID-19 pandemic, *Research in International Business and Finance*, Vol. 54. https://doi.org/10.1016/j.ribaf.2020.101248.

Demir, Ender, Giray Gozgor, Chi K. M. Lau, and Samuel A. Vigne (2018). Does economic policy uncertainty predict the Bitcoin returns? An empirical investigation, *Finance Research Letters*, **26**, pp. 145–149.

Goodell, John W. (2020). COVID-19 and finance: Agendas for future research, *Finance Research Letters*, Vol. 35. https://doi.org/10.1016/j.frl.2020.101512.

Goodell, John W. and Goutte, S. (2020). Co-movement of COVID-19 and Bitcoin: Evidence from wavelet coherence analysis, *Finance Research Letters*, Vol. 38. https://doi.org/10.1016/j.frl.2020.101625.

Goutte, Stéphane, Khaled Guesmi, and Samir Saadi. (2019). "Cryptofinance and mechanisms of exchange: The making of virtual currency", Springer Edition.

Grinsted, Aslak, John C. Moore, and Svetlana Jevrejeva (2004). Application of the cross wavelet transform and wavelet coherence to geophysical time series, *Nonlinear Processes in Geophysics*, **11**.

Kang, Sang H., Ron P. McIver, and Jose A. Hernandez (2019). Co-movements between Bitcoin and Gold: A wavelet coherence analysis, *Physica A*, **536**.

Klein, Tony, Hien P. Thu, and Thomas Walther (2018). Bitcoin is not the New Gold – A comparison of volatility, correlation, and portfolio performance, *International Review of Financial Analysis*, **59**, pp. 105–116.

Kurka, Josef (2019). Do cryptocurrencies and traditional asset classes influence each other?, *Finance Research Letters*, **31**, pp. 38–46.

Matkovskyy, Roman and Akanksha Jalan (2019). From financial markets to Bitcoin markets: A fresh look at the contagion effect, *Finance Research Letters*, **31**, pp. 93–97.

Raza, Syed A., Nida Shah, and Muhammad Shahbaz (2018). Does economic policy uncertainty influence gold prices? Evidence from a nonparametric causality-in-quantiles approach, *Resources Policy*, **57**, pp. 61–68.

Smales, Lee A. (2019). Bitcoin as a safe haven: Is it even worth considering?, *Finance Research Letters*, **30**, pp. 385–393.

Wang, Gang-Jin, Chi Xie, Danyan Wen, and Longfeng Zhao (2019). When Bitcoin meets economic policy uncertainty (EPU): Measuring risk spillover effect from EPU to Bitcoin, *Finance Research Letters*, **31**, pp. 489–497.

Wu, Shan, Mu Tong, Zhongyi Yang, and Abdelkader Derbali (2019). Does gold or Bitcoin hedge economic policy uncertainty? *Finance Research Letters*, **31**, pp. 171–178.

Chapter 4

Energy, Environment, and Financial Markets Under the COVID-19 Pandemic

Hela Mzoughi[*,‡] and Christian Urom[†,§]

*University of Tunis Carthage-Carthage Business School,
R.U. Economic and Statistical Modelling and Analysis-Higher
School of Statistics and Information Analysis, Tunis, Tunisia
†Paris School of Business, 54 Rue Nationale,
Paris, France
‡hela.mzoughi@utctunisie.com
§sainturom@gmail.com

We examine the impact of COVID-19 pandemic on oil prices, CO_2 emissions, and stock market volatility. We demonstrate that although the increasing number of COVID-19 infections caused a decrease in the price of crude oil, the negative response of the oil market is short-lived. However, the response of economic activities as measured by CO_2 emissions persists. Also, we find a stronger impact on equity market volatility than on crude oil prices and CO_2 emissions. Lastly, the share of error variance in CO_2 emissions is stronger than that of the energy and stock markets. Taken together, our findings shed light on the depth of the impact of COVID-19 on the environment, and the energy and financial markets.

Keywords: Oil Price, COVID-19, CO2 Emissions, Financial Volatility, VIX

1. Introduction

The growing COVID-19 pandemic and the uncertainty in crude oil markets continue to stress the business cycle of the local and global economy. The negative global demand shock and supply–demand imbalances are a significant threat to the oil market. The coronavirus pandemic is also connected with global energy consumption which is linked to the reduction of toxic materials such as CO_2. In this study, we investigate the impact of crude oil price on carbon emission for recent business cycles under the COVID-19 pandemic and financial volatility.

Our research deals mainly with two strands of the literature review. The first focused on the relationship between energy (oil) price and energy consumption, as a vital element for economic growth. For instance, Leng Wong *et al.* (2013), Mensah *et al.* (2019), Al-Mulali and Ozturk (2016), Li *et al.* (2019), and Ohler and Billger (2014), among others, found a negative relationship between energy (oil) prices and energy consumption. They suggested that a rise in oil price leads to a reduction in the consumption of oil, thus these results are in favor of lower carbon emissions. Within the climate change context, CO_2 emission is the main cause of global warming. Indeed, climate variables can also be a direct cause of biological interactions between Severe Acute Respiratory Syndrome (SARS) and humans. Optimal temperature, humidity, and wind speed are variables that can determine the survival and transmission of the SARS virus (Yuan *et al.*, 2006). Recently, Tosepu *et al.* (2020) analyzed the correlation between weather and COVID-19 pandemic in Jakarta, Indonesia. The components of weather included minimum temperature (°C), maximum temperature (°C), temperature average (°C), humidity (%), and amount of rainfall (mm). The results affirmed that the weather factor is one of the factors that triggered the spread of COVID-19 (SARS-CoV-2). This brings to mind how Greenhouse Gases can contribute to further risk towards the pandemic's propagation.

The second strand of the literature focused on the relationship between oil prices and financial volatility. Within this framework, Illing and Liu (2006) pointed out a positive correlation between the level of financial stress and oil price shocks was proved in the Canada context. On the other hand, Das *et al.* (2018) considered the dependence between stock prices, commodity prices, and financial stress and involved a bilateral causality between oil prices and financial volatility in the US context. This finding converged with the research outcomes of Basher and Sadorsky (2015). Indeed, the authors pointed out the hedging property of oil prices and volatility index (VIX), for emerging markets' stock prices. A recent working paper from Albulescu (2020) examined how new COVID-19 infections affect oil prices, while controlling for the role of financial stress and VIX, and the economic policy uncertainty of the United States using an Autoregressive Distributed Lag (ARDL) specification. The results showed that COVID-19 daily report of cases of new infections have a marginal negative impact on the crude oil prices in the long-run; but the effect on the recent dynamics is indirect.

Despite the interesting idea, the author neglected the different interactions between variables, and since COVID-19 is a pneumatic disease, the effect of climate change deserves to be considered. Therefore, we fill this gap and test the impact of COVID-19 on oil prices emphasizing the role of CO_2 emissions, while controlling the role of VIX using an unrestricted vector autoregression (VAR). We demonstrate that although COVID-19 pandemic caused a decrease in the price of crude oil, the negative response of the oil market is short-lived. However, the response of economic activities as measured by CO_2 emissions is negative throughout the study period. Also, we find a stronger impact on equity market volatility than on crude oil prices and CO_2 emissions. Lastly, we find that the share of forecast error variance in the level of CO_2 emissions is stronger than that of the energy and stock markets.

2.   Empirical Strategy

When it's time to create the Table of Contents or Index that spans the entire project, and perhaps ensuring that all the page numbers are consecutive, RD fields are the most stable mechanism in Word for this purpose. With predefined TOC and Index fields present at the master template, TOC and index entries are automatically generated using these Macros. In the empirical analysis we perform an unrestricted VAR analysis to explain the effects of the current COVID-19 infections on the energy market, economic activities, and the stock markets. This method of analysis allows us to test for the endogeneity of all variables and the responses of oil prices, emissions, and stock returns to COVID-19 infection shocks in order to capture the short-run dynamics of the variables. The reduced-form VAR specification estimated in this study is defined by the following dynamic equation:

$$Y_t = \gamma_0 + \sum_{i=1}^{p} \gamma_i Y_{t-i} + \varepsilon_t$$

where Y_t is the vector of variables and γ_0 is a column vector of the constant term, p is the number of lags. $Y_t = [Y_{1t} \dots Y_{kt}]'$ represents a column vector of all the variables in the model (crude oil prices, COVID-19 number of confirmed cases of infections, CO_2 emissions, and stock market VIX) whereas γ_i is a $k \times k$ matrix of unknown coefficients. ζ_t is a column vector of errors.

Data on COVID-19 infected cases are extracted from the daily situation reports by World Health Organization, whereas the oil price data are from the U.S. Energy Information Administration.[1] For the CO_2 emissions, we collect from the International Energy Agency reports the average consumption of crude oil. Then, we calculate the approximate amount of CO_2 emitted and estimate the whole vector using the "Temporal disaggregation" using the Chow and Lin (1973) method. The Chicago Board Options Exchange (CBOE) VIX was retrieved from FRED database. Our sample covers the period January 22, 2020–March 30, 2020 (69 observations). Table 1 shows the descriptive statistics and unit root test, while Fig. 1 shows the plots of these variables over the study period.

The correlations between COVID-19 infections and oil prices, and CO_2 emissions are negative, implying that as infection increased, oil prices and CO_2 emissions decreased. Together, these show that as infections increased, economic activities decreased (as implied by reductions in CO_2 emissions), and leading to a fall in demand for crude oil and, therefore, fall in oil prices. Also, both oil prices and CO_2 emissions have a strong negative relation with the equity market volatility. A plausible explanation here is that as economic activities pick up, demand for crude oil increases, leading to increase in oil prices. Increasing oil prices and economic activities decrease equity

---

[1] https://www.eia.gov.

Table 1: Descriptive statistics and ADF unit root tests.

Variable	Mean	Std. Dev.	ADF(level)	ADF(1st diff)
Oil	42.95	11.72	$-1.628(0.7821)$	$-6.432^*(0.0000)$
InfCOVID	136250	164820	$-5.079^*(0.0001)$	$-4.712^*(0.002)$
CO_2	42864000	347040	$-2.045(0.5618)$	$-6.098^*(0.0003)$
VIX	35.73	22.69	$-1.319(0.8829)$	$-8.504^*(0.0000)$
	Oil	InfCOVID	CO_2	VIX
Oil	1			
InfCOVID	-0.832	1		
CO_2	0.864	-0.785	1	
VIX	-0.934	0.688	-0.843	1

Note: *denotes value significant at 1% level.

market volatility. However, the positive correlation between infections and VIX indicates that as confirmed cases increase, restrictions in both movements and economic activities lead to increase in volatility due to increased uncertainty.

3. Results and Discussion

The output from our estimation is presented in terms of impulse response functions and variance decomposition as presented in Fig. 2 and Table 2, respectively. Following past studies (see e.g., Giordano *et al.*, 2007; Diaz and de Gracia, 2017), we constructed the impulse responses with the assumption that a shock equals 1% of confirmed number of COVID-19 infections. In all cases, results show that the impulse responses of crude oil prices, CO_2 emissions, and stock market volatility to a standard deviation shock on COVID-19 infection are statistically significant. With particular reference to the energy market, the impulse response function shown in Fig. 2(a) indicates that a positive shock to the number of COVID-19 infections causes a decrease in the price of crude oil during the impact period. After the impact period, the impact on the oil market becomes positive and this shock dies out around the 9th day. The implication of this result is that the negative response of oil prices to an increase in the number of COVID-19 infections is short-lived. The size of this shock is about -1.6%. The size of this shock diminishes towards the end of the first day. It is also notable that whereas the response of the energy market becomes positive after the first period, the size of

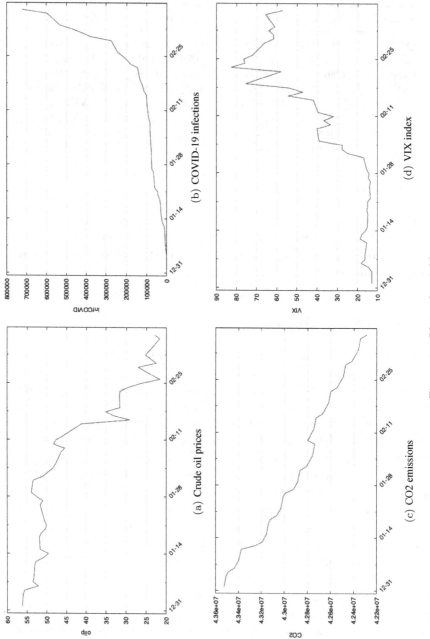

Figure 1:   Plots of variables.

Table 2:　Variance decomposition.

Days	DLInfCOVID	DCO_2	DOILP	DVIX
Oil prices				
1	3.824	4.425	91.75	0.000
3	8.204	3.633	86.13	5.779
5	8.361	5.215	79.13	7.29
7	8.132	6.291	77.26	8.298
10	8.212	6.312	77.22	8.257
CO_2 emissions				
1	16.34	83.66	0.000	0.000
3	15.81	81.43	1.957	0.808
5	18.82	75.68	4.658	0.836
7	20.12	72.88	5.495	1.504
10	20.25	72.43	5.638	1.683
VIX index				
1	1.905	36.84	3.416	57.83
3	9.599	29.49	9.733	51.17
5	10.86	26.3	14.82	48.02
7	11.05	26.79	14.33	47.82
10	11.19	26.41	14.91	47.49
COVID-19 infections				
1	100	0.000	0.000	0.000
3	86.77	5.633	7.008	0.583
5	83.15	8.216	6.756	1.881
7	82.06	7.996	6.735	3.184
10	80.91	8.232	7.432	3.421

the positive response is significantly lower throughout the remaining periods than the negative response, implying a negative net impact of COVID-19 infections on oil prices. This confirms the findings of past studies, including Albulescu (2020).

As shown in Fig. 2(b), the response of economic activities as measured by CO_2 emissions to a shock on COVID-19 infections is negative throughout the horizon and decays around the 10th period. The statistically significant negative response of CO_2 emissions to COVID-19 infections implies that as the number of infections increases, the decisions of many countries to implement the lock-down on movement and shutdown most production activities

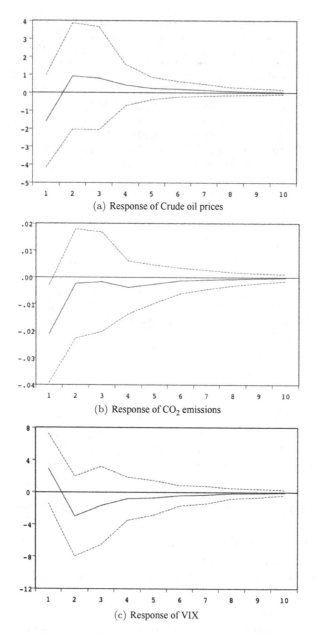

(a) Response of Crude oil prices

(b) Response of CO_2 emissions

(c) Response of VIX

Figure 2: Plots of impulse response functions to COVID-19 shock.

tend to decrease the emissions of harmful substances into the atmosphere. This result is particularly in concordance with Cheze *et al.* (2020), who found that the deep economic recession in 2008–2009 was a leading cause of the emissions' reductions during the period from 2008–2012. In a broader sense, it also lends credence to the existing consensus among energy policy-makers concerning the harmful effect of the current global energy mix in which the fossil fuel-based energy consumption due to increased economic activities contribute significantly to CO_2 emissions (see e.g., Le *et al.*, 2020).

In Fig. 2(c), the response of global equity market VIX is significantly positive during the impact period but becomes negative afterwards until it dies out during the 9th day. Concerning the size of impact, although the impact becomes negative after the first period, the COVID-19 pandemic appears to have had a stronger impact on equity market volatility than on crude oil prices and CO_2 emissions. The positive response of equity market volatility to COVID-19 pandemic is well documented in literature given that as the number of infected persons increase, preventive actions taken by many countries including lock-down and restrictions in movement lead to declining economic activities. The uncertainty created by this situation leads to increase in stock market volatility due to declining investors' confidence. The decrease in stock market volatility after the impact of a shock on COVID-19 pandemic is attributable to the news of economic relief programs which appear to have increased stock prices by reducing investors' risk aversion and improved projections on long-term growth (Gormsen and Koijen, 2020).

As noted earlier, we present the forecast error variance decomposition estimates up to the 10th day for the respective variables in Table 2. For the energy market, we find that COVID-19 pandemic explains about 3.8% of forecast error variance in crude oil prices in the first day. The forecast power of the pandemic increases to about 8.4% in the fifth day but declines slightly to 8.2%. With regards to CO_2 emissions, in the first day, COVID-19 pandemic explains about 16.3% of error variance in CO_2 emissions. The size of the share of error variance due to the pandemic increases to about 20.3% in the tenth day. This result implies that the share of error variance in CO_2 emissions due to the pandemic is greater than that of the energy market. This is understandable due to the substantial reduction in the level of CO_2 emissions following the recent lock-down and declining global economic activities.

The share of the pandemic on the variance error in stock market VIX increases from about 1.9% to 11.2% in the first day and tenth day, respectively. This shows a significant increase in the share of the pandemic on the error variance of the VIX index as the number of infections increases. Lastly, it is not unexpected that the error variance decomposition for the pandemic shows evidence of persistence with the share of variance due to its past value remaining high (80.9%) up till the tenth day. It is also not unlikely that CO_2 emissions explain about 8.2% of the error variance in the number of COVID-19 infections. This is due to the fact that the coronavirus is a respiratory disease and its spread and fatality may not be unconnected with the availability of toxic materials such as CO_2 emissions.

4. Conclusion

In this chapter, we have explored the impact of COVID-19 pandemic on oil prices, CO_2 emissions, and stock market volatility over the period January 22, 2020–March 30, 2020 using an unrestricted VAR. Our results demonstrate that although COVID-19 pandemic caused a decrease in the price of crude oil, the negative response of the oil market is short-lived. However, the response of economic activities as measured by CO_2 emissions is negative throughout the forecast period. Also, we find a stronger impact on equity market volatility than on crude oil prices and CO_2 emissions. Lastly, we find that the share of forecast error variance in the level of CO_2 emissions is stronger than that of the energy and stock markets. Our results shed light on the impact of the current global economic situation created by the COVID-19 pandemic. We note that although economic activities seem to be picking up in China where the outbreak began, the ravaging impacts of the pandemic are still very high in most parts of the world especially Europe and North America. In the light of this, collaborative efforts in economic intervention to speed up economic recovery and boost investor' perception of long-term growth are required.

References

Al-Mulali, U. and Ozturk, I. (2016). The investigation of environmental Kuznets curve hypothesis in the advanced economies: The role of energy prices, *Renewable and Sustainable Energy Reviews*, **54**, pp. 1622–1631.

Albulescu, C. (2020). Coronavirus and oil price crash, *Working Papers hal02507184, HAL*.

Basher, S. A. and Sadorsky, P. (2015). Hedging emerging market stock prices with oil, gold, VIX, and bonds: A comparison between DCC, ADCC and GO-GARCH, *Energy Economics*, **54**, pp. 235–247.

Cheze, B., Chevallier, J., Berghmans, N., and Alberola, E. (2020). On the CO_2 emissions determinants during the EU ETS phases I and II: A plant-level analysis merging the EUTL and Platts power data, *The Energy Journal*, **41**, pp. 153–184.

Chow, G. and Lin, A. (1973). Best linear unbiased interpolation, distribution, and extrapolation of time series by related series, *The Review of Economics and Statistics*, **53**, pp. 372–375.

Das, D., Kumar, S., Tiwari, A., Shahbaz, M., and Hasim, H. (2018). On the relationship of gold, crude oil, stocks with financial stress: A causality-in-quantiles approach, *Finance Research Letters*, **27**, pp. 169–174.

Diaz, E. M. and de Gracia, F. P. (2017). Oil price shocks and stock returns of oil and gas corporations, *Finance Research Letters*, **20**, pp. 75–80.

Giordano, R., Momigliano, S., Neri, S., and Perotti, R. (2007). The effects of fiscal policy in Italy: Evidence from a VAR model, *European Journal of Political Economy*, **23**, pp. 707–733.

Gormsen, N. J., Koijen, R. S. J. and Roussanov, N. (2020). Coronavirus: Impact on Stock Prices and Growth Expectations, *The Review of Asset Pricing Studies*, **10**, pp. 574–597.

Illing, M. and Liu, Y. (2006). Measuring financial stress in a developed country: An application to Canada, *Journal of Financial Stability*, **2**, pp. 243–265.

Le, T. H., Chang, Y., and Park, D. (2020). Renewable and nonrenewable energy consumption, economic growth, and emissions: International evidence, *The Energy Journal*, **41**, pp. 73–92.

Leng Wong, S., Chia, W.-M., and Chang, Y. (2013). Energy consumption and energy R&D in OECD: Perspectives from oil prices and economic growth, *Energy Policy*, **62**, pp. 1581–1590.

Li, K., Fang, L., and He, L. (2019). How population and energy price affect China's environmental pollution? *Energy Policy*, **129**, pp. 386–396.

Mensah, I. A., Sun, M., Gao, C., Omari-Sasu, A. Y., Zhu, D., Ampimah, B. C., and Quarcoo, A. (2019). Analysis on the nexus of economic growth, fossil fuel energy consumption, CO_2 emissions and oil price in Africa based on a PMG panel ARDL approach, *Journal of Cleaner Production*, **228**, pp. 161–174.

Ohler, A. M. and Billger, S. M. (2014). Does environmental concern change the tragedy of the commons? Factors affecting energy saving behaviors and electricity usage. *Ecological Economics*, **107**, pp. 1–12.

Tosepu, R., Gunawan, J., Effendy, D., Ahmad, L. A. I., Lestari, H., Bahar, H., and Asfian, P. (2020). Correlation between weather and COVID-19 pandemic in Jakarta, Indonesia, *Science of the Total Environment*, **725**, p. 138436.

Yuan, J., Yun, H., Lan, W., Wang, W., S.-G., S., and Jia, S. (2006). A climatologic investigation of the SARS-CoV outbreak in Beijing, China, *American Journal of Infection Control*, **34**, pp. 234–236.

Chapter 5

Gold and Bitcoin are Safe-haven? Evidence from Developed and Emerging Market Indices During the COVID-19 Bear Market

Hana Belhadj[*,**] **and Salah Ben Hamad**[†,‡]

*University of Sfax, Tunis
†Université de Tunis El Manar, Tunis
**belhadjhana1@gmail.com
‡benhamad_salah@yahoo.fr

In this study, we compare the role and the safe-haven properties of bitcoin and gold against developed and emerging market indices during extreme market conditions as the COVID-19 crisis. We explore the effects of adding bitcoin and gold to an optimal portfolio by relying Sharpe ratio and genetic algorithm approach. We use a stochastic dominance approach to compare the performance of portfolios for each scenario. The results show that by adding bitcoin, the portfolio performance improves only during the sovereign debt crisis. However, during the non-crisis period and during the COVID-19 crisis, the portfolios with and without bitcoin do not dominate, this shows that bitcoin does not act as a safe-haven. However, our results affirm the safe-haven nature of gold during the COVID-19 crisis.

Keywords: COVID-19, Bitcoin, Gold, Safe Haven, Developed Markets, Emerging Markets

1. Introduction

In this study, we will explore the ability of bitcoin as well as gold in diversifying developed and emerging portfolios, as well as their safe-haven abilities during times of high uncertainty such as the COVID-19 crisis. Indeed, the bear market resulting from the COVID-19 pandemic provides a first testing ground for bitcoin's safe-haven properties. Bitcoin's selection is based on its ability to generate abnormal returns, while gold presents itself as an effective hedging investment opportunity in financial portfolios.

After the financial turmoil of the last decade, investors continue to seek alternative investment vehicles that offer diversification and/or hedging advantages. As was the case with commodities in the early 2000s, and due to its high average return and low correlation with major financial assets, Bitcoin could be a useful tool for portfolio management. In this context, Tully and Lucey (2007), Dyhrberg (2016) show that Bitcoin could serve as a hedging tool against the US dollar in the short term. Using wavelet and quantile regression, Bouri *et al.* (2017a) study the hedging behavior of Bitcoin by analyzing a positive relationship between Bitcoin and global uncertainty.

Likewise, Bouoiyour and Selmi (2017) argue that Bitcoin exhibits the properties of a safe-haven in the short and long term. In the same vein, Bouri *et al.* (2017b) argue that bitcoin was like a shelter against sovereign risk and the fragility of the global financial system. This was demonstrated during the euro area sovereign crisis of 2010–2013 (Luther and Salter, 2017). The fact is that bitcoin is isolated from economic and financial variables (Corbet *et al.*, 2018). This is especially so in times of market downturn (Briére *et al.*, 2015). Similarly, in 2012, the European Central Bank concluded that cryptocurrencies do not jeopardize financial stability, due to their limited link to the real economy.

On the other hand, several empirical studies refute the safe-haven role of Bitcoin during the recent crisis of the COVID-19 pandemic. Indeed, the COVID-19 pandemic crisis, which began in late December 2019, provides a first testing ground to verify Bitcoin's safe-haven properties. In this context, Conlon and McGee (2020) conducted an empirical study, in which they want to test the safe-haven role of Bitcoin during the COVID-19 crisis as well. Their results show that Bitcoin does not act as a safe-haven asset. Indeed, Bitcoin rather increases the risk of the portfolio containing only the S&P500

index. Hence, these results cast doubt on the safe-haven capacity of Bitcoin during times of crisis. These results are confirmed by Kristoufek (2010).

Section 2 presents the database and its descriptive statistics. Section 3 explains the methodology. In Section 4, we present and discuss our results. Section 5 concludes.

2. Data Presentations and Descriptive Analyses

The dataset that we study consists of the price values of Bitcoin, Lingot, and the main developed and emerging stock market index (Cac40, Dax, Ibex35, S&P500, Ftse100, Nikkei225, Shanghai index, Ftse Brazil, Nifty50, and MOEX). Our sampling period is from March 2012 to May 2020. We use the monthly prices obtained from DataStream and the site fr.investing.com.

The timeframe of our variables is limited by the availability of Bitcoin prices. In fact, monthly historical price data for Bitcoin is available from March 2012 on the site fr.investing.com. For each time series, we have 98 monthly observations. The historical price of Bitcoin is plotted in Fig. 1. The prices of the various assets have been transformed into returns. According to the publication of the BNP Paribas bank and according to the work of Corbet *et al.* (2020), our study period (March 2012 to May 2020) is divided into three subperiods: period of sovereign debt crisis (March 2012 to June 2013), stable period (July 2013 to December 2019), and period of crisis caused by the COVID-19 pandemic (January 2020 to May 2020).

Table 1 provides descriptive statistics of all assets used in portfolio optimization during the sovereign debt crisis. During the sovereign crisis, according to the average results, bitcoin is the best performing

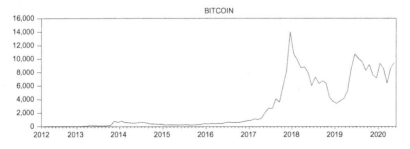

Figure 1: Evolution of the price of Bitcoin in US dollars.

Table 1:   Descriptive statistics of data during the sovereign crisis.

| | During the Sovereign Crisis | | | | | |
	Average	SD	Skewness	Kurtosis	JB	Prob
Bitcoin	19.93%	31.26%	1.05	4.34	3.9	0.1422
Gold	−1.69%	4.84%	−0.74	2.32	1.68	0.43
Cac40	0.58%	3.86%	−0.822	2.38	1.92	0.38
Dax	0.90%	3.57%	−1.033	3.45	2.79	0.24
Ibex35	0.20%	7.87%	−0.043	2.77	0.03	0.98
S&P500	0.87%	2.79%	−1.081	4.30	3.98	0.13
Ftse100	0.49%	13%	−1.026	7.40	14.78	0.0006
Nikkei225	2.03%	5.92%	−0.465	2.72	0.58	0.74
Shanghai	−0.89%	6.71%	0.1385	3.44	0.16	0.91
FTSE brazil	−1.18%	4.12%	−1.039	3.38	2.79	0.24
Nifty50	0.65%	4.11	0.114	2.51	0.18	0.91
MOEX	−1.41%	3.23%	−0.758	7.43	13.72	0.001

(19.93%). In contrast, gold and IBEX 35 have the lowest average performance. For the standard deviation, bitcoin returns are more volatile than the other assets (31.26%).

For the asymmetry coefficient (skewness), the flattening coefficient of the distribution (kurtosis), and the test for normality (JarqueBera (JB)) displayed in Table 1, the results of all variables follow the normal distribution during the period of sovereign crisis with the exception of the FTSE 100 and MOEX index.

Table 2 provides descriptive statistics of all assets during the non-crisis period. During the non-crisis period, bitcoin is the best performing asset associated with very high volatility (29.14%). The asymmetry coefficient (skewness), the flattening coefficient of the distribution (kurtosis), and the test for normality (JB) displayed in Table 2 show that the distribution of the returns of all the considered assets are not normal, except for Cac40, Dax, Ibex35, Ftse Brazil, and Nifty50.

We display the descriptive statistic of data during the COVID-19 pandemic crisis in Table 3. During the crisis of the COVID-19 pandemic, all assets have averaged negative returns except for gold and bitcoin. In fact, during this recent crisis, all the stock market indices studied suffered a significant drop in their average returns and an increase in their volatilities. The COVID-19 crisis has a strong positive impact on the volatility of each stock market

Table 2: Descriptive statistics of data during the non-crisis period.

	During the non-crisis period					
	Average	SD	Skewness	Kurtosis	JB	Prob
Bitcoin	5.51%	29.14%	2.30	15.09	544.25	0.000
Gold	0.40%	3.65%	0.62	4.58	13.27	0.001
Cac40	0.60%	3.90%	−0.14	2.58	0.83	0.66
Dax	0.65%	4.14%	−0.22	2.54	1.31	0.51
Ibex35	0.26%	4.34%	−0.13	2.82	0.34	0.84
S&P500	0.89%	3.26%	−0.68	4.03	9.52	0.008
Ftse100	0.24%	3.63%	−0.15	5.06	14.10	0.0008
Nikkei225	0.70%	4.96%	−0.66	3.16	5.83	0.053
Shanghai	0.55%	3.67%	0.15	35.99	3583.970	0.000
FTSE brazil	0.85%	5.65%	−0.07	2.76	0.25	0.87
Nifty50	0.94%	3.89%	−0.08	2.65	0.49	0.78
MOEX	0.62%	5.90%	−0.34	4.53	9.22	0.0099

Table 3: Descriptive statistics of data during the COVID19 pandemic crisis.

	During the COVID19 pandemic crisis				
	Average	SD	Skewness	Kurtosis	JB
Bitcoin	5.42%	24.46%	−0.37	1.66	0.48
Gold	3.52%	5.01%	−0.40	2.11	0.29
Cac40	−4.83%	9.36%	−0.59	1.96	0.51
Dax	−2.68%	11.05%	−0.30	1.69	0.43
Ibex35	−5.93%	11.39%	−1.11	2.68	1.05
S&P500	−1.18%	10.13%	0.053	1.65	0.37
Ftse100	−4.32%	8.17%	−0.21	1.46	0.52
Nikkei225	−1.56%	8.78%	0.028	1.29	0.60
Shanghai	−1.13%	3.33%	0.77	2.25	0.61
FTSE brazil	−5.57%	17.95%	−0.91	2.43	0.76
Nifty50	−4.48%	14.37%	−0.35	2.46	0.16
MOEX	−2.49%	12.80%	−0.84	2.35	0.68

(Corbet *et al.*, 2020). Bitcoin has also suffered a decrease in its average return from 5.51% to 5.42%. Whereas gold is the only asset that has seen a significant increase in its average return. Its average yield goes from 0.40% to 3.52%. For standard deviation, gold returns are less volatile than bitcoin and the other indexes. This shows the safe-haven characteristic of gold during unstable periods. Regarding the skewness coefficient, the flattening coefficient of the distribution (kurtosis), and the JB test (JB) displayed in Table 3, all the assets studied are Gaussian.

3. Methodology

In this study, we focus our analysis on the effect of Bitcoin as an investment asset while comparing it with gold. Thus, in order to assess the role of bitcoin in emerging and developed portfolios during three sub periods: during the sovereign debt crisis of the euro zone, during the stable period, and during the crisis of the COVID-19 pandemic, we are building six types of portfolios.

- Portfolio 1 (P1) is made up of developed stock market index.
- Portfolio 2 (P2) is made up of developed stock market index + bitcoin.
- Portfolio 3 (P3) is made up of developed stock market index + gold (ingot).
- Portfolio 4 (P4) is made up of emerging stock market index.
- Portfolio 5 (P5) is made up of emerging stock market index + bitcoin.
- Portfolio 6 (P6) is made up of emerging stock market index + gold.

Our analysis takes place according to two scenarios:

- 1st scenario: We will optimize the six types of portfolios by maximizing the Sharpe ratio. After that, we will apply the stochastic dominance method in order to compare two by two the optimal portfolios (P1, P2), (P1, P3), (P4, P5), and (P4, P6) for the three sub periods.
- 2nd scenario: We are going to apply a method based on artificial intelligence, namely, genetic algorithm, which allows us to assign the optimal weights to each asset to obtain optimal portfolios. Then, we use the stochastic dominance method which allows to compare (P1 with P2), (P1 with P3), (P4 with P5), and (P4 with P6) during the crisis periods and the non-crisis period.

Models for portfolio optimization

Instead of focusing on the efficient frontier of the mean-variance (MV), we seek to optimize the portfolio Sharpe ratio (SR) (Sharpe, 1966).

The Sharpe ratio combines information from the mean and variance of an asset.

It's pretty straightforward, and it's a risk-adjusted measure of average return, which is often used to assess a portfolio's performance. It is described with the following equation:

$$\text{Sh} = \frac{R_i - R_f}{\sigma_i} \tag{1}$$

where

Sh: Sharpe ratio,

R_i: mean return of portfolio i,

R_f: return of the risk-free asset,

σ_i: the standard deviation of R_i.

By adjusting the optimal weights, we will balance the trade-off between maximizing the expected return and minimizing risk in order to maximize the Sharpe ratio. The Sharpe ratio is used in this study to find an optimal portfolio.

Presentation of genetic algorithms and their applications in finance

The genetic algorithm GA is stochastic search technique based on the mechanisms of natural selection and genetics proposed for the first time by John Holland (1975). They are based on the principles of survival of the most suitable structures and exchange of information. At each generation, a new set of artificial creatures (encoded as strings) is constructed from the best elements of the previous generation. Although relying heavily on chance (and therefore on a random number generator) these algorithms are not purely random.

In recent years, there has been a boom in the application of genetic algorithms to solve the problem of multi-objective optimization known as scalable multi-objective optimization or genetic multi-objective optimization. The fundamental characteristic of genetic algorithms is the multidirectional and global search, in which a population of potential solutions is maintained from generation to generation.

Numerous studies have shown that GA can efficiently find optimal or even optimal solutions for many combinatorial optimization problems. Such as the study of Soleimani *et al.* (2009).

Soleimani *et al.* (2009)'s experiences show that the proposed GAs are applicable and reliable in real markets with a large number of assets.

Pereira (2000) argues that genetic algorithms are a valid approach for many practical problems in finance that can be complex and therefore require the use of an efficient and robust optimization technique. Some applications of genetic algorithms to complex financial market problems include: yield forecasting, portfolio optimization, trading rule discovery, and optimization of trading rules. In addition, Dai *et al.* (2009) reported that GAs show promising results in financial applications and that GAs are effective for portfolio issues.

Optimization by genetic algorithm

A genetic algorithm is an iterative method of finding the optimal solution. It manipulates a population of constant size. This population consists of candidate points called chromosomes. This algorithm leads to a phenomenon of competition between chromosomes. Each chromosome is the encoding of a potential solution to the problem to be solved, it consists of a set of elements called genes, which can take several values. At each iteration (generation), a new population is created with the same size. This generation consists of the best chromosomes "adapted" to their environment, represented by the selective function. Gradually, the chromosomes tend towards the optimum of the selective function. Convergence to a chromosome of high physical activity is done through genetic algorithm operators (selection, crossing, and mutation).

The genetic algorithm randomly begins with a population generation "k".

Three genetic operations (selection, crossing, and mutation) are repeated for the elements of the population "k" in order to move to a second generation "$k + 1$".

Beginning with the first genetic operation, that is, the selection, which optimizes the objective function by selecting the relevant elements.

The cross is the main genetic operator. It operates on two parents (chromosomes) at a time and generates two new chromosomes by combining the two characteristics of the "parent" chromosomes.

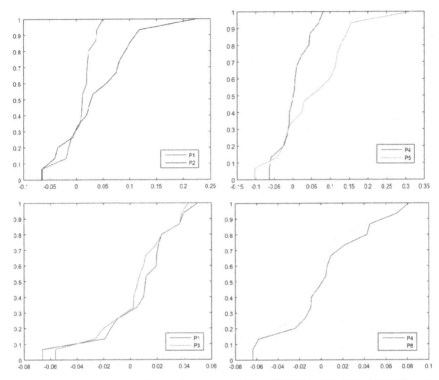

Figure 2: Plot of the CDFs of the two portfolios (P1,P2), (P1,P3), (P4,P5), and (P4,P6) during sovereign period.

In the case of weight selection problem, the crossing plays the role of exchanging weights of the securities that make up the portfolio. There are some forms of crossing: one point, two points, multipoint, and uniform.

Finally, mutation is a background operator that produces spontaneous random changes in various chromosomes. Mutation is used to maintain the diversity of individuals in a population in order to prevent the premature convergence of solutions. A crossover operation creates new, remote individuals in the search space of their parent individuals. Therefore, the mutation operation can be considered as a small perturbation on the chromosomes of an individual that improves the exploration of the search space. Figure 2 illustrates the different operations involved in a basic genetic algorithm.

Basic Genetic Algorithm

Initialize a population generated randomly.
Assessment: Assess the physical condition of each chromosome
  in the population
Calculation of the selective function
  Repeat
  Selection
Crossing
Mutation
Calculation of the selective function
Until the stop criterion is met

The mathematical formulation of the objective function in a GA application

This subsection introduces the problem of multiobjective portfolio optimization and MOGA's approach to solve this problem.

The evaluation is performed using the objective function which depends on the specific problem and the optimization objective of the genetic algorithm (Petridis *et al.*, 1998). The objective is to determine the optimal proportions associated with each asset to maximize returns and minimize portfolio risk. The mathematical model, which is an expanded form of the Markowitz MV approach, is presented as follows:

$$Min \ \delta_p^2(w) = \sum_{i=1}^{n} \sum_{j=1}^{n} w_i w_j \sigma_{ij} \tag{2}$$

$$Max \ r_p(w) = \sum_{i=1}^{n} \mu_i w_i \tag{3}$$

Under constraints: $\sum_{i=1}^{n} w_i = 1$ and $w_i \geq 0$, $i = 1, \ldots, n$

δ_p^2: Portfolio variance;

r_p: the return of the portfolio;

σ_{ij}: the covariance between the returns of assets i and j;

w_i: the weight of each asset in the portfolio;

μ_i: the average yield of assets i.

$$\tag{4}$$

Normally, single objective optimization aims to find an optimal overall solution, however, multi-objective optimization aims to find a set of Pareto optimal overall solutions. Therefore, there are two conflicting objectives to optimize. In this study, the problem of optimizing multi-objective portfolios is formulated as follows:

$$Min\, H(w) = \delta_p^2(w) - r_p(w) \tag{5}$$

constraints: $\sum_{i=1}^{n} w_i = 1$ et $w_i \geq 0$, $i = 1, \ldots, n$

Fitness function

The fitness function is another important aspect of GA for solving optimization problems. In optimizing asset allocation, the fitness function must make a rational compromise between risk reduction and maximizing returns. Thus, it can be designed as follows:

$$Min\, H(w) = \delta_p^2(w) - r_p(w) \tag{6}$$

constraints: $\sum_{i=1}^{n} w_i = 1$ and $w_i \geq 0$, $i = 1, \ldots, n$.
The fitness function of each chromosome is the indicator that allows GA to make the selection.

Stochastic dominance

According to Markowitz (1952), investors optimally estimate efficient portfolios by minimizing risk, as measured by standard deviation, for a desired level of return or maximizing returns for a given level of risk. Markowitz (1952) MV model is frequently used to control risk and assess portfolios. The main criticism of this model is that it assumes the normality of the distribution of returns, which is not always the case. For this purpose, if the distribution of returns is not normal, the results could be biased and misleading.

To overcome the limitations of the MV approach, academics suggest adopting the rules of DS stochastic dominance, developed by Hadar and Russell (1969), and others. The main advantage of using this approach is that it provides a very general framework for evaluating portfolio selection without the need for asset price benchmarks. In addition, it is based on less restrictive assumptions than the MV method, satisfies the general utility function, and takes into account all distribution information in the comparison of two risks. Whereas the MV approach takes into account only the first two moments, the DS approach has been considered one of the most useful tools for classifying investment perspectives (see, for e.g., Levy, 1992). Several authors have applied stochastic dominance, such as Abid *et al.* (2014), who used the stochastic dominance method to compare the performance of two national and international portfolios. Meyer *et al.* (2005) use DS criteria to examine whether the inclusion of foreign assets in a domestic portfolio generates diversification benefits. Similarly, Lean *et al.* (2015) apply the stochastic dominance method to determine whether gold performs well for the diversification of French portfolios.

Let X and Y be two real random variables, with their cumulative distribution functions (CDFs) F_x and F_y and their probability density functions (PDFs) f_x and f_y, respectively, defined on the common support $[n, m]$ with $n < m$. We define:

$$H0 = h \quad \text{and} \quad H_j(a) = \int_n^a H_{j-1}(t)dt. \tag{7}$$

For $h = f_x$, f_y, $H = F_x$, F_y and $j = 1, 2, 3$.

The most widely used stochastic dominance (SD) rules are: first-order stochastic dominance "FSD", second-order stochastic dominance "SSD" and third-order stochastic dominance "TSD". All investors are non-satiated (i.e., prefer higher returns to less) under FSD, non-satiated and risk-averse under SSD, and non-satiated, risk-averse, and possessing decreasing absolute risk aversion (DARA) under TSD.

We define the fact that X is stochastically dominated by Y at order 1, noted $X \prec^{st1} Y$, as follows: $X \prec^{st1} Y \longleftrightarrow F_{x1} \geq F_{y1} \longleftrightarrow F_{x1}(a) \geq F_{y1}(a)$ for all possible returns, a ϵ $[n, m]$ with a strict inequality for some a. Stochastic dominance at order 1 will only be valid if the CDFs of the alternatives do not intersect. We can say that if X is stochastically dominated by Y at order 1 if there is an arbitrage opportunity between X and Y so that investors will increase their expected wealth, as well as their expected utility, if their investments are spent from X to Y. On the other hand, if FSD does not exist between X and Y, we can conclude that the markets are efficient and investors are rational.

We define the fact that X is stochastically dominated by Y at order 2, noted $X \prec^{st2} Y$, as follows: $X \prec^{st2} Y \longleftrightarrow F_{x2} \geq F_{y2} \longleftrightarrow$

$F_{x2}(a) \geq F_{y2}(a)$ for all possible returns $a \, \epsilon \, [n, \, m]$ with a strict inequality for some a. In this case, the two distribution functions of X and Y intersect. Indeed, for any possible value of a, the air under F_{x2} is larger than that under F_{y2}.

We define the fact that X is stochastically dominated by Y at order 3, noted $X \prec^{st3} Y$, as follows: $X \prec^{st3} Y \longleftrightarrow F_{x3} \geq F_{y3} \longleftrightarrow F_{x3}(a) \geq F_{y3}(a)$ for all possible returns $a \, \epsilon \, [n, m]$ with a strict inequality for some a.

We note that there is a hierarchical relationship in stochastic dominance. FSD implies SSD, which, in turn, implies TSD. However, the opposite is not true: the existence of SSD does not imply the existence of FSD. Likewise, the existence of TSD does not imply the existence of SSD or FSD.

There are two main classes of Stochastic Dominance tests: one is the minimum/maximum statistic (Barrett and Donald, 2003; Linton et al. (2005)), and the other is based on distribution values calculated on a set of grid points (DD) (Davidson and Duclos (2000)). Since the DD test is one of the most powerful tests, we apply it in our analysis.

For two assets X and Y with their CDFs F_x and F_y, respectively, and for a grid of pre-selected points $a_1, a_2, \ldots, a_k$, the order-j DD statistic, $T_j(a)$ ($j = 1, 2$ and 3), is:

$$\hat{T}_j(a) = \frac{\hat{F}_{xj}(a) - \hat{F}_{yj}(a)}{\sqrt{\hat{V}_j(a)}}, \tag{8}$$

where

$$\hat{V}_j(a) = \hat{V}_x^j(a) + \hat{V}_y^j(a) - 2\hat{V}_{x,y}^j(a),$$

$$\hat{H}_j(a) = \frac{1}{N(j-1)!} \sum_{i=1}^{N} (a - h_i)_+^{j-1},$$

$$\hat{V}_H^j(a) = \frac{1}{N} \left[\frac{1}{N((j-1)!)^2} \sum_{i=1}^{N} (a - h_i)_+^{2(j-1)} - \hat{H}_j(a)^2 \right],$$

$$H = F_x, \; F_y \text{ and } h = x, y,$$

$$\hat{V}_{x,y}^j(a) = \frac{1}{N}\left[\frac{1}{N((j-1)!)^2}\sum_{i=1}^{N}(a-x_i)_+^{j-1}(a-y_i)_+^{j-1}\right.$$

$$\left. - \hat{F}_{xj}(a)\hat{F}_{yj}(a)\right].$$

In which F_x and F_y are defined in (1) and $(a)_+ = \max\{a, 0\}$.

It is empirically impossible to test the null hypothesis for the total support of the distributions. Thus, we test the null hypothesis for a preconceived finite number of values a. Specifically, the following hypotheses are tested:

H0: $F_{xj}(a_i) = F_{yj}(a_i)$ for all a_i, $i = 1, 2, \ldots, k$,

HA: $F_{xj}(a_i) \neq F_{yj}(a_i)$ for some a_i,

HA1: $F_{xj}(a_i) \leq F_{yj}(a_i)$ for all a_i, $F_{xj}(a_i) < F_{yj}(a_i)$ for some a_i,

HA2: $F_{xj}(a_i) \geq F_{yj}(a_i)$ for all a_i, $F_{xj}(a_i) > F_{yj}(a_i)$ for some a_i

To control the probability of rejecting the null hypothesis, following Bishop, Formby, and Thistle (1992) (BFT), we use the Studentized Maximum Modulus (SMM) distribution with m and infinite degrees of freedom, noted M_∞^k. The percentile $1 - \alpha$ of M_∞^k, noted $M_\infty^k\alpha$, is tabulated by Stoline and Ury (1979) and the following decision rules are adopted:

if $|T_s(a_i)| < M_{\infty\alpha}^k$ for $i = 1, \ldots, k$, "accept H0";
if $T_s(a_i) < M_{\infty,\alpha}^k$ for all i and $-T_s(a_i) > M_{\infty,\alpha}^k$ for some i, "accept HA1";
if $-T_s(a_i) < M_{\infty,\alpha}^k$ for all i and $T_s(a_i) > M_{\infty,\alpha}^k$ for some i, "accept HA2";
if $T_s(a_i) > M_{\infty,\alpha}^k$ for all i and $-T_s(a_i) > M_{\infty,\alpha}^k$ for some i, "accept HA".

The DD test compares the distributions at a finite number of grid points $\{a_k,\ k = 1, 2, \ldots, k\}$. The choice of these points is guided by the results of various studies. Tse and Zhang (2004) show that the appropriate choice of k for reasonably large samples is between 6 and 15. In this case, too few grids will miss information on the distributions between any two consecutive grids (Barrett and Donald, 2003).

We note that in the above hypotheses, HA is excluded from both HA1 and HA2, which means that if either HA1 or HA2 is accepted, it does not mean that HA is accepted. Accepting either H0 or HA implies that there are no SD relationships and no arbitrage opportunity between these two diversified portfolios and neither of these two portfolios is preferred to the other. However, if HA1 or HA2 is accepted in the first order, this shows that a P1 portfolio stochastically dominates a P2 portfolio at the first order. In this situation, there is an arbitrage opportunity and, as a result, investors can maximize their expected wealth if they move from the dominated portfolio to the dominant one. On the other hand, if HA1 or HA2 is accepted according to the second or third order, we say that P1 stochastically dominates P2 at the second or third order. In this situation, an arbitrage opportunity does not exist and the transition from one portfolio to another will only increase the expected utility of investors, but not their expected wealth (Wong *et al.*, 2008).

4. Empirical Results

Tables 4–9 illustrate the optimal weights of the six portfolios, obtained by maximizing the Sharpe ratio.

From Tables 4 and 5, we see that including bitcoin in a portfolio, containing developed stock indices, increases the return. In fact, the return of the portfolio goes from 0.78% to 2.10%. Likewise, the risk of the portfolio increases by adding bitcoin, it goes from 0.13% to 0.48%. From Tables 4 and 6, we see that adding gold to a portfolio of developed indices results in a decrease in the risk and return of the portfolio. Indeed, the risk goes from 0.13% to 0.10%.

According to Tables 7 and 8, for the average returns of the portfolios, we note that there is a clear increase of 2.2% for the portfolio including bitcoin compared to the one which is composed only by the emerging stock indices of the BRIC countries. For the risk, the portfolio including bitcoin is more volatile than the one without bitcoin. The variance goes from 0.24% for P4 to 1% for P5.

Tables 7 and 9 show that by adding gold to the portfolio of emerging indices, the risk has been significantly reduced from 0.24% to 0.14%.

Table 4:   The optimal weights of the different assets of the portfolio P1.

ACTIFS	FTSE100	IBEX35	CAC40	DAX	Nikkei225	S&P500
W	0	0	0	0	0.03223	0.9677

Average return = 0.0078
Variance = 0.00139

Table 5:   The optimal weights of the different assets of the portfolio P2.

ACTIFS	FTSE100	IBEX35	CAC40	DAX	Nikkei225	S&P500	BITCOIN
W	0	0	0	0	0	0.8092	0.1907

Average return = 0.021
Variance = 0.0048

Table 6:   The optimal weights of the different assets of the portfolio P3.

ACTIFS	FTSE100	IBEX35	CAC40	DAX	Nikkei225	S&P500	GOLD
W	0	0	0	0	0.0773	0.7704	0.1522

Average return = 0.00704
Variance = 0.00103

Table 7:   The optimal weights of the different assets of the portfolio P4.

ACTIFS	MOEX	FTSE BRAZIL	NIFTY50	SHANGHAI
W	0	0	1	0

Average return = 0.0060
Variance = 0.0024

Table 8:   The optimal weights of the different assets of the portfolio P5.

ACTIFS	MOEX	FTSE BRAZIL	NIFTY50	SHANGHAI	BITCOIN
W	0	0	0.6903	0	0.3096

Average return = 0.0280
Variance = 0.01

Table 9:   The optimal weights of the different assets of the portfolio P6.

ACTIFS	MOEX	FTSE BRAZIL	NIFTY50	SHANGHAI	Gold
W	0	0	0.72918	0	0.2708

Average return = 0.0050
Variance = 0.0014

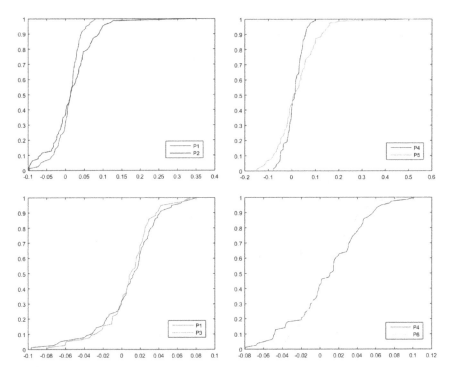

Figure 3:   Plot of the CDFs of the two portfolios (P1 P2), (P1,P3), (P4,P5), and (P4,P6) during the non-crisis period.

4.1.   Dominance stochastic

From Figs. 3–5, we find that for the three sub periods, the CDFs of (P1, P2), (P1, P3), (P4, P5), and (P4, P6) cross. It is therefore clear that there is no first-order stochastic domination (DS) between the pairs during the three sub periods.

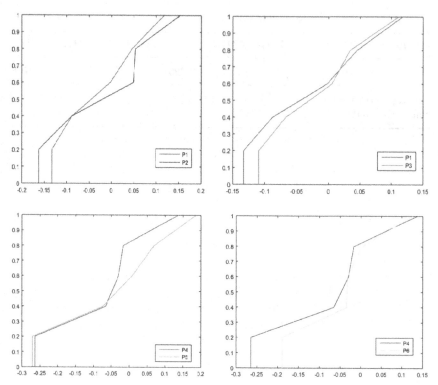

Figure 4:   Plot of the CDFs of the two portfolios (P1 P2), (P1,P3), (P4,P5), and (P4,P6) during the COVID-19 pandemic crisis.

From Table 10, regarding developed markets, we notice that the portfolio P2 (with bitcoin) dominates the one without bitcoin P1 at the second and third-orders during the sovereign debt crisis. However, during the non-crisis period and during the COVID-19 crisis, this dominance disappeared. This means that bitcoin does not provide a diversification benefit and it is a poor hedge during downturns.

Table 10 also reveals the absence of a second- and third-order stochastic dominance between portfolios with and without gold during the non-crisis period for developed markets. We note that during the sovereign crisis in the euro zone, portfolios without gold dominate those with gold. While during the COVID-19 crisis, the portfolio P3 (with gold) dominates the portfolio P1 at the second and third order. Which means it's best for risk-averse agents to add gold to

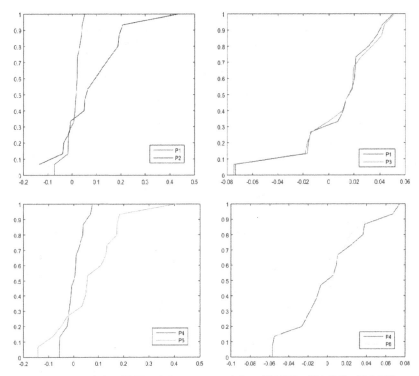

Figure 5: Plot of the CDFs of the two portfolios (P1 P2), (P1,P3), (P4,P5), and (P4,P6) during the sovereign crisis.

their developed portfolios during the recent crisis, to maximize their expected utility.

From Table 11, regarding emerging markets, we see that the P5 portfolio (with bitcoin) dominates the portfolio P4 at the second and third order during the sovereign debt crisis. However, during the non-crisis period and during the COVID-19 crisis, this dominance disappeared. This means that bitcoin is neither a safe-haven nor a hedge against the extreme bear market in the emerging countries occasioned by the COVID-19 pandemic.

Table 11 also reveals the absence of the second- and third-order stochastic dominance between portfolios with and without gold during the non-crisis period for emerging markets. We note that during the sovereign crisis in the euro zone, portfolios without gold dominate those with gold. While during the COVID-19 crisis, the portfolio P6 (with gold) dominates the portfolio P4 according to the

Table 10:   Stochastic dominance test between P1, P2, and P3.

	During the sovereign crisis	During the non-crisis period	During the COVID-19 pandemic crisis
	P1	**P1**	**P1**
P2 (with bitcoin)	$\succ^{2,3}$	**ND**	**ND**
P3 (with gold)	$\prec^{2,3}$	**ND**	$\prec^{2,3}$

Note: $\succ$ means that P2 or P3 dominates P1, $\prec$ means that P3 dominates P1. ^{2,3} means SSD and TSD. ND means that there is no SD. The significance level of all our SD tests is the conventional one, which is 5%.

Table 11:   Stochastic dominance test between P4, P5, and P6.

	During the sovereign crisis	During the non-crisis period	During the COVID-19 pandemic crisis
	P4	**P4**	**P4**
P5 (with bitcoin)	$\succ^{2,3}$	**ND**	**ND**
P6 (with gold)	$\prec^{2,3}$	**ND**	$\succ^{2,3}$

Note: $\succ$ means that P5 or P6 dominates P4, $\prec$ means that P6 dominates P4. ^{2,3} means SSD and TSD. ND means that there is no SD. The significance level of all our SD tests is the conventional one, which is 5%.

second and third order. Which means it's best for risk-averse agents to add gold to their emerging portfolios during the recent crisis, in order to maximize their expected utility.

According to the 1st scenario, when the six types of portfolios have been optimized by maximizing the Sharpe ratio, the results of stochastic dominance reveal that:

Emerging and developed portfolios including bitcoin stochastically dominate those without bitcoin at the second and third orders during the sovereign crisis. This implies that risk averse investors would be better off by including bitcoin in their portfolios in order to maximize their expected utilities. However, during the stable period and during the COVID-19 crisis, this dominance disappeared, showing that investors have no interest to add bitcoin in their portfolios. This proves that bitcoin cannot be considered a safe-haven during

Table 12:   The optimal weights of the different assets of the portfolio P1.

ACTIFS	FTSE100	IBEX35	CAC40	DAX	Nikkei225	S&P500
W	0.0043	0.012	0.0135	0.0404	0.1343	0.7965

Value of the objective function = −0.0061
Variance = 0.0014
Average return = 0.0076

Table 13:   The optimal weights of the different assets of the portfolio P2.

ACTIFS	FTSE100	IBEX35	CAC40	DAX	Nikkei225	S&P500	BITCOIN
W	0.0372	0.0037	0.0156	0.3601	0.1272	0.0467	0.4104

Value of the objective function = −0.0182
Variance = 0.0149
Average return = 0.035

times of high uncertainty for developed and emerging markets. These results are confirmed by Conlon and McGee (2020).

> Regarding gold, we found that during the sovereign crisis, emerging and developed portfolios including gold are dominated by portfolios without gold at the second and third orders. While, during the recent COVID-19 crisis, portfolios with gold dominate those without gold at the second and third orders. This proves that gold is found to be a safe-haven from market turbulence. This conclusion is confirmed by the study of Akhtaruzzman (2020).

Tables 12–17 illustrate the optimal weights of the six portfolios, obtained by the genetic algorithms. From Tables 12 and 13, we see that including bitcoin in a portfolio, containing developed stock indices, results in an increase in returns. In fact, the return of the portfolio goes from 0.76% to 3.5%. Likewise, the risk of the portfolio increases by adding bitcoin, it goes from 0.14% to 1.49%.

From Tables 12 and 14, we see that by adding gold to a portfolio containing developed indices, the risk of the portfolio decreases from 0.0014 to 0.0013.

According to Tables 15 and 16, concerning the average returns of the portfolios, we see that there is a clear increase of 2.8% for the

Table 14:   The optimal weights of the different assets of the portfolio P3.

ACTIFS	FTSE100	IBEX35	CAC40	DAX	Nikkei225	S&P500	GOLD
W	0.0101	0.0025	0.001	0.0101	0.2524	0.666	0.0582

Value of the objective function $= -0.0061$
Variance $= 0.0023$
Average return $= 0.0057$

Table 15:   The optimal weights of the different assets of the portfolio P4.

ACTIFS	MOEX	FTSE BRAZIL	NIFTY50	SHANGHAI
W	0.0524	0.0184	0.9121	0.0161

Value of the objective function $= -0.0034$
Variance $= 0.0023$
Average return $= 0.0057$

Table 16:   The optimal weights of the different assets of the portfolio P5.

ACTIFS	MOEX	FTSE BRAZIL	NIFTY50	SHANGHAI	BITCOIN
W	0.085	0.1465	0.3097	0.0552	0.4046

Value of the objective function $= -0.0171$
Variance $= 0.0166$
Average return $= 0.0337$

portfolio containing bitcoin compared to the one containing only the emerging stock market indices of BRIC countries. For the risk, the portfolio including bitcoin is more volatile than the one without bitcoin. The variance goes from 0.23% for the P4 to 1.66% for the P5. Tables 15 and 17 show that by adding gold to the portfolio of emerging indices, the risk decreases slightly from 0.23% to 0.22%.

From Figs. 5–7, we see that the CDFs of (P1, P2), (P1, P3), (P4, P5), and (P4, P6) intersect for the three sub periods. It is therefore clear that there is no first-order stochastic dominance (DS) between each peer for the three sub periods.

From Table 18, we note that during the sovereign debt crisis, portfolio P2 (including bitcoin) dominates portfolio P1 (without bitcoin)

Table 17: The optimal weights of the different assets of the portfolio P6.

ACTIFS	MOEX	FTSE BRAZIL	NIFTY50	SHANGHAI	GOLD
W	0.0836	0.0448	0.7671	0.0127	0.0916

Value of the objective function = −0.0032
Variance = 0.0022
Average return = 0.0052

at the second and third orders. This means that risk-averse investors prefer to include bitcoin in their portfolios in order to maximize their expected utility during the crisis period. This means that bitcoin can be a safe-haven for developed markets during the sovereign debt crisis. However, during the non-crisis period, the two portfolios P1 and P2 do not dominate. In addition, our results reveal that the refuge character of bitcoin disappeared during the crisis period of the COVID-19 pandemic, indeed, during this recent crisis the P1 and P2 did not dominate, which shows that investors have no interest to add bitcoin in their portfolio. Regarding gold, we note that during the sovereign crisis and during the crisis of the COVID-19 pandemic, the portfolio including gold dominates the one without gold at the second and third orders for developed markets. This means that investors should add gold to their portfolios in order to maximize their expected utility. This confirms the safe-haven role of gold for developed markets during times of crisis. However, this dominance disappeared during the non-crisis period. Indeed, during the non-crisis period, portfolios without gold and with gold do not dominate.

Table 19 reveals the existence of a stochastic dominance at the second and third order between P4 and P5 during the sovereign debt crisis. However, this dominance disappeared during the crisis of the COVID-19 pandemic. It can be concluded that bitcoin cannot act as a safe-haven for emerging markets during unstable times. For the non-crisis period, the portfolios P5 and P4 do not dominate. This shows that bitcoin cannot provide a diversification benefit.

Regarding gold, we see from Table 19 that there is no stochastic dominance between P4 and P6 during the non-crisis period. While during the sovereign crisis, the portfolio without gold dominates that

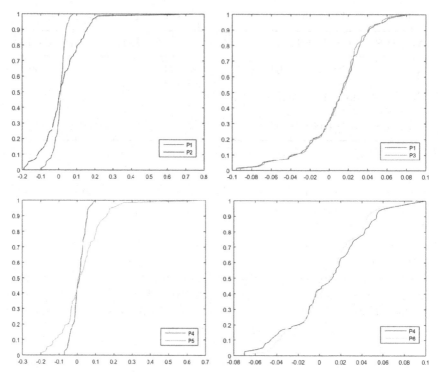

Figure 6:   Plot of the CDFs of the two portfolios (P1 P2), (P1,P3), (P4,P5), and (P4,P6) during the non-crisis period.

with gold. However, during the recent crisis caused by the COVID-19 pandemic, the portfolio including gold dominates the one without gold, proving that gold can be considered as a safe-haven asset for emerging markets during times of high uncertainty.

According to the 2nd scenario, by applying the method of genetic algorithms to optimize the six types of portfolios, the results of the stochastic dominance method reveal that for developed and emerging markets, portfolios including bitcoin stochastically dominate those without bitcoin at the second and third orders only during the sovereign crisis. While, during the crisis of the COVID-19 pandemic, this dominance disappeared. This proves that bitcoin cannot be used as a safe-haven asset during times of turbulence. During the non-crisis period, portfolios with and without bitcoin do not dominate for developed and emerging markets. Our empirical finding cast doubt on the ability of bitcoin to provide shelter from turbulence. These results

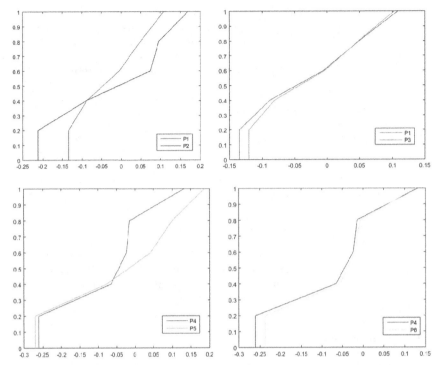

Figure 7: Plot of the CDFs of the two portfolios (P1 P2), (P1,P3), (P4,P5), and (P4,P6) during the COVID-19 pandemic crisis.

are confirmed by Conlon and McGee (2020) who indicated that in times of severe financial and economic disruption, cryptocurrencies do not serve as a hedge or a safe-haven, but rather can be amplifiers of contagion.

Regarding gold, we find that there is no dominance between the portfolio with and without gold only during the period of the COVID-19 pandemic crisis for emerging markets. Indeed, during this crisis the portfolio with gold dominates that without gold, which proves that during periods of serious financial and economic disturbances, gold acts as a safe-haven asset. However, for developed markets, the gold wallet dominates the goldless one during the sovereign crisis and during the crisis of the COVID-19 pandemic. This confirms the safe-haven role of gold. The increase in gold prices during this crisis can be explained by global travel restrictions and supply chain disruptions impacting its supply.

Table 18:   Stochastic dominance test between P1, P2, and P3.

	During the sovereign crisis	During the non-crisis period	During the COVID-19 pandemic crisis
	P1	**P1**	**P1**
P2 (with bitcoin)	$\succ^{2,3}$	ND	ND
P3 (with or)	$\prec^{2,3}$	ND	$\succ^{2,3}$

Note: $\succ$ means that P2 or P3 dominates P1 means that P1 dominates P2 or P3. ^{2,3} means SSD and TSD, respectively. ND means that there is no SD. The significance level of all our SD tests is the conventional one, which is 5%.

Table 19:   Stochastic dominance test between P4, P5, and P6.

	During the sovereign crisis	During the non-crisis period	During the COVID-19 pandemic crisis
	P4	**P4**	**P4**
P5 (with bitcoin)	$\succ^{2,3}$	ND	ND
P6 (with or)	$\prec^{2,3}$	ND	$\succ^{2,3}$

Note: $\succ$ means that P5 or P6 dominates P4. $\prec$ means that P4 dominates P6. ^{2,3} means SSD and TSD. ND ND means that there is no SD. The significance level of all our SD tests is the conventional one, which is 5%.

5.   Conclusion

We conducted a comparative study between bitcoin and gold, studying their roles as factors of diversification, and to determine if they serve as a safe-haven for developed and emerging markets during times of crisis like the COVID-19 crisis. Indeed, the bear market resulting from the COVID-19 pandemic provides a first testing ground for bitcoin's safe-haven properties.

The empirical results show that under both scenarios, developed and emerging portfolios including bitcoin dominate those without bitcoin only during the sovereign debt crisis. However, during the non-crisis period and during the COVID-19 crisis, this dominance disappeared, this shows that Bitcoin does not act as a safe-haven. Regarding gold, the results show that for developed and emerging markets, portfolios with gold and without gold do not dominate during the non-crisis period, while, during the COVID-19 crisis, portfolios with gold dominate those without gold at the second and third orders. This finding affirms the safe-haven nature of gold. These results are aligned with the results found by Kristoufek (2010).

References

Abid, F., Leung, P. L., Mroua, M., and Wong, W. K. (2014). International diversification versus domestic diversification: Mean-variance portfolio optimization and stochastic dominance approaches. *Journal of Risk and Financial Management*, **7**(2), pp. 45–66.

Barrett, G. F. and Donald, S. G. (2003). Consistent tests for stochastic dominance. *Econometrica*, **71**(1), pp. 71–104.

Bouoiyour, J. and Selmi, R. (2017). The Bitcoin price formation: Beyond the fundamental sources. arXiv preprint, arXiv:1707.01284.

Bouri, E., Gupta, R., Tiwari, A. K., and Roubaud, D. (2017a). Does Bitcoin hedge global uncertainty? Evidence from wavelet-based quantile-in-quantile regressions. *Finance Research Letters*, **23**, pp. 87–95.

Bouri, E., Jalkh, N., Molnár, P., and Roubaud, D. (2017b). Bitcoin for energy commodities before and after the December 2013 crash: Diversifier, hedge or safe-haven? *Applied Economics*, **49**(50), pp. 5063–5073.

Briere, M., Oosterlinck, K., and Szafarz, A. (2015). Virtual currency, tangible return: Portfolio diversification with bitcoin. *Journal of Asset Management*, **16**(6), pp. 365–373.

Conlon, T. and McGee, R. (2020). Safe haven or risky hazard? Bitcoin during the COVID-19 bear market. *Finance Research Letters*, **35**, p. 101607.

Corbet, S., Meegan, A., Larkin, C., Lucey, B., and Yarovaya, L. (2018). Exploring the dynamic relationships between cryptocurrencies and other financial assets. *Economics Letters*, **165**, pp. 28–33.

Corbet, S., Larkin, C., and Lucey, B. (2020). The contagion effects of the COVID-19 pandemic: Evidence from gold and cryptocurrencies. *Finance Research Letters*, **35**, p. 101554.

Dai, C., Chen, W., Zhu, Y., and Zhang, X. (2009). Seeker optimization algorithm for optimal reactive power dispatch. *IEEE Transactions on Power Systems*, **24**(3), pp. 1218–1231.

Davidson, R. and Duclos, J.-Y. (2000). Statistical inference for stochastic dominance and for the measurement of poverty and inequality. *Econometrica*, **68**(6), pp. 1435–1464.

Dyhrberg, A. H. (2016). Hedging capabilities of Bitcoin. Is it the virtual gold? *Finance Research Letters*, **16**, pp. 139–144.

Hadar, J. and Russell, W. (1969). Rules for ordering uncertain prospects. *American Economic Review*, **59**, pp. 25–34.

Holland, J. (1975). Adaptation dans les systèmes naturels et artificiels: une analyse introductive avec application à la biologie. *Contrôle et Intelligence Artificielle*.

Kristoufek, L. (2020). Grandpa, grandpa, tell me the one about Bitcoin being a safe-haven: Evidence from the COVID-19 pandemics. arXiv preprint, arXiv:2004.00047.

Lean, H. H. and Wong, W. K. (2015). Is gold good for portfolio diversification? A stochastic dominance analysis of the Paris stock exchange. *International Review of Financial Analysis*, **42**, pp. 98–108.

Levy, H. (1992). Stochastic dominance and expected utility: survey and analysis. *Management Science*, **38**(4), pp. 555–593.

Luther, W. J. and Salter, A. W. (2017). Bitcoin and the bailout. *The Quarterly Review of Economics and Finance*, **66**, pp. 50–56.

Markowitz, H. (1952). Portfolio selection, *Journal of Finance*, **7**, pp. 77–91.

Meyer, T., Li, X., and Rose, L. (2005). Comparing mean variance tests with stochastic dominance tests assessing international portfolio diversification benefits. *Financial Services Review*, **14**, pp. 149–168.

Pereira, R. (2000). Genetic algorithm optimisation for finance and investments. MPRA Paper 8610, University Library of Munich, Germany.

Petridis, V., Kazarlis, S., and Bakirtzis, A. (1998). Varying fitness functions in genetic algorithm constrained optimization: The cutting stock and unit commitment problems. *IEEE Transactions on Systems, Man, and Cybernetics, Part B (Cybernetics)*, **28**(5), pp. 629–640.

Soleimani, H., Golmakani, H. R., and Salimi, M. H. (2009). Markowitz-based portfolio selection with minimum transaction lots, cardinality constraints and regarding sector capitalization using genetic algorithm. *Expert Systems with Applications*, **36**(3), pp. 5058–5063.

Sharpe, W. F. (1966). Mutual fund performance. *The Journal of Business*, **39**(1), pp. 119–138.

Stoline, M. R. and Ury, H. K. (1979), Tables of the studentized maximum modulus distribution and an application to multiple comparisons among means. *Technometrics*, **21**, pp. 87–93.

Tse, Y. and Zhang, X. (2004). A Monte Carlo investigation of some tests for stochastic dominance. *Journal of Statistical Computation and Simulation*, **74**(5), pp. 361–378.

Tully, E. and Lucey, B. M. (2007). A power GARCH examination of the gold market. *Research in International Business and Finance*, **21**(2), pp. 316–325.

Wong, W.-K., Phoon, K. F., and Lean, H. (2008). Stochastic dominance analysis of Asian hedge funds. *Pacific-Basin Finance Journal*, **16**(3), pp. 204–223.

Annexes

Optimization by maximizing the Sharpe ratio

P1

	rend	poids	covariance	ftse100	IBEX35	cac40	dax	nikkei225	s&p500		
ftse100	0,000531	0	ftse100	0,003829	0,001324	0,001204	0,001376	0,00121	0,00114	rend	0,0078663
IBEX35	-0,001233	0	IBEX35	0,001324	0,003084	0,002071	0,001996	0,001877	0,001344	ecartype	0,0372824
cac40	0,003223	0	cac40	0,001204	0,002071	0,001914	0,001808	0,00157	1,21E-03	var	0,00139
dax	0,00522	0	dax	0,001376	0,001996	0,001808	0,00209	0,001679	0,001313		
nikkei225	0,007904	0,0322363	nikkei225	0,00121	0,001877	0,00157	0,001679	0,002806	0,001351	Sharpe	0,1774635
s&p500	0,007865	0,9677637	s&p500	0,00114	0,001344	0,001208	0,001313	0,001351	0,001391		
	somme	1									

P2

	rend	poids	covariance	ftse100	IBEX35	cac40	dax	nikkei225	s&p500	BTC		
ftse100	0,000531	0		ftse100	0,003829	0,001324	0,001204	0,001376	0,00121	0,00114	0,005237	rend	0,0210921
IBEX35	-0,001233	0	ftse100	0,003829	0,001324	0,001204	0,001376	0,00121	0,00114	0,005237	ecartype	0,069341327
cac40	0,003223	0	IBEX35	0,001324	0,003084	0,002071	0,001996	0,001877	0,001344	0,001742	var	0,00480822
dax	0,00522	0	cac40	0,001204	0,002071	0,001914	0,001808	0,00157	1,21E-03	0,001818		
nikkei225	0,007904	0	dax	0,001376	0,001996	0,001808	0,00209	0,001679	0,001313	0,002898	Sharpe	0,28615114
s&p500	0,007865	0,8092043	nikkei225	0,00121	0,001877	0,00157	0,001679	0,002806	0,001351	0,00408		
BTC	0,077191	0,1907957	s&p500	0,00114	0,001344	0,001208	0,001313	0,001351	0,001391	0,002502		
	somme	1	btc	0,005237	0,001742	0,001818	0,002898	0,00408	0,002502	0,085839		

P3

	rend	poids	covariance	ftse100	IBEX35	cac40	dax	nikkei225	s&p500	gold		
ftse100	0,000531	0		ftse100	0,003829	0,001324	0,001204	0,001376	0,00121	0,00114	4,11E-05	rend	0,007041899
IBEX35	-0,001233	0	ftse100	0,003829	0,001324	0,001204	0,001376	0,00121	0,00114	4,11E-05	ecartype	0,032103487
cac40	0,003223	0	IBEX35	0,001324	0,003084	0,002071	0,001996	0,001877	0,001344	-1,08E-04	var	0,001030634
dax	0,00522	0	cac40	0,001204	0,002071	0,001914	0,001808	0,00157	1,21E-03	2,57E-05		
nikkei225	0,007904	0,0773348	dax	0,001376	0,001996	0,001808	0,00209	0,001679	0,001313	1,08E-05	Sharpe	0,180413388
s&p500	0,007865	0,7704416	nikkei225	0,00121	0,001877	0,00157	0,001679	0,002806	0,001351	-0,000485		
gold	0,002438	0,1522235	s&p500	0,00114	0,001344	0,001208	0,001313	0,001351	0,001391	6,15E-06		
	somme	1	gold	4,11E-05	-1,08E-04	2,57E-05	1,08E-05	-0,000485	6,15E-06	0,001604		

P4

	rend	poids	covariance	Moexfn	ftse brazil	NIFTY50	shanghai index		
Moexfn	0,001523	0		Moexfn	ftse brazil	NIFTY50	shanghai index	rend	0,006037
ftse brazil	0,00214	0	Moexfn	0,018493	0,001126	0,000672	0,002103	ecartype	0,0493255
NIFTY50	0,006037	1	ftse brazil	0,001126	0,004307	0,001723	0,002377	var	0,002433
shanghai ind	0,002363	0	NIFTY50	0,000672	0,001723	0,002433	0,001109		
	somme	1	shanghai ind	0,002103	0,002377	0,001109	0,106779	Sharpe	0,0970493

P5

	rend	poids	covariance	Moexfn	ftse brazil	NIFTY50	shanghai ind	BTC		
Moexfn	0,001523	0		Moexfn	ftse brazil	NIFTY50	shanghai ind	BTC	rend	0,0280717
ftse brazil	0,00214	0	Moexfn	0,018493	0,001126	0,000672	0,002103	0,003014	ecartype	0,1002951
NIFTY50	0,006037	0,6903254	ftse brazil	0,001126	0,004307	0,001723	0,002377	0,002855	var	0,0100591
shanghai ind	0,002363	0	NIFTY50	0,000672	0,001723	0,002433	0,001109	1,56E-03		
BTC	0,0771914	0,3096746	shanghai ind	0,002103	0,002377	0,001109	0,106779	0,007237	Sharpe	1,5549513
	somme	1	BTC	0,003014	0,002855	1,56E-03	0,007237	0,085839		

P6

	rend	poids	0	covariance									
Moexfn	0,001523	0			Moexfn	ftse brazil	NIFTY50	shanghai ind:	gold				
ftse brazil	0,00214	0		Moexfn	0,018493	0,001126	0,000672	0,002103	0,000185		rend	0,0050623
NIFTY50	0,006037	0,7291858		ftse brazil	0,001126	0,004307	0,001723	0,002377	0,000221		ecartype	0,037614
shanghai ind:	0,002363	0		NIFTY50	0,000672	0,001723	0,002433	0,001109	8,91E-06		var	0,0014148
GOLD	0,002438	0,2708142		shanghai ind:	0,002103	0,002377	0,001109	0,106779	0,002206			
	somme		1	gold	0,000185	0,000221	8,91E-06	0,002206	0,001604			
										Sharpe	0,1013543	

Optimization by genetic algorithms

P1

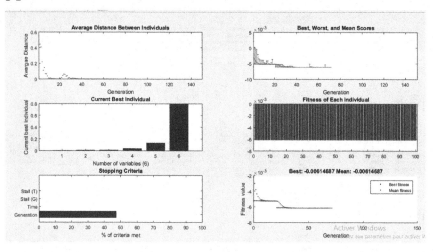

P2

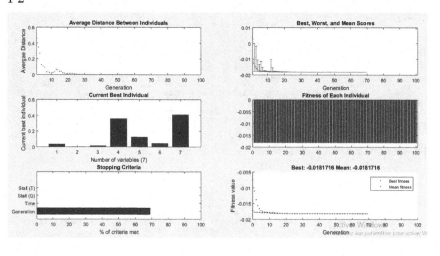

P3

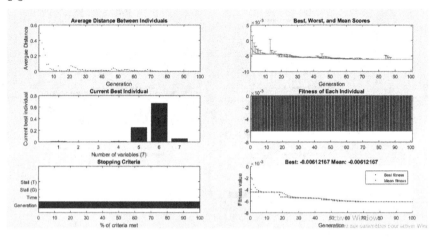

P4

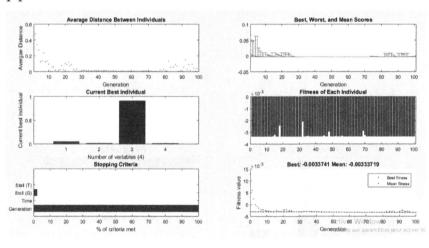

P5

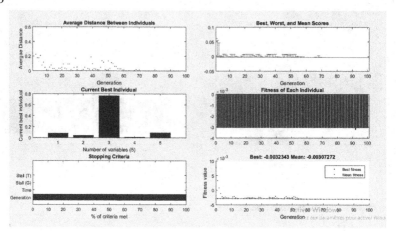

P6

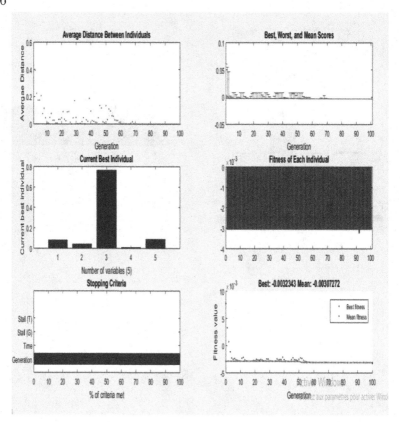

Chapter 6

COVID-19 Pandemic Haunting the Energy Market: From the First to the Second Wave

Donia Aloui* and Rafla Hchaichi[†]

*Carthage Business School, University of Tunis Carthage,
Tunis 2036, Tunisia*
*donia.aloui@utctunisie.com
[†] rafla.hchaichi@utctunisie.com

By using the structural VAR model with time-varying coefficients, this chapter aims to assess the impact of COVID-19 shocks on crude oil and natural gas S&P GSCI during the first wave and to compare it to that during the second wave. The findings confirm that S&P GS indices' responses to COVID-19 shock are varying over time. This variation in responses can be explained by the unstable behavior of investors in an extremely uncertain environment. We find that the energy market remains vulnerable to the surge in coronavirus deaths, during the second wave, even though the damage on oil prices is less than that of the first wave. Our results show that the negative effect on the natural gas index worsens over time and becomes substantial with the arrival of the second wave.

Keywords: COVID-19, Oil Price War, Health Crisis, Drop Oil Price, S&P GS Commodity Index, TVP-SVAR Model, Crude Oil, Natural Gas

1. Introduction

For a long time, oil has been considered the engine of the world's economy. Crude oil, or so-called "black gold", is considered one of the world's most precious commodities that affect the global economy as well as world trade. However, crude oil prices are prone to booms and drops. Previously, supply shortages had been generating dramatic fluctuations in oil prices, such as the Iranian revolution, the Iran–Iraq war, the Arab oil embargo, the Gulf wars, and the Asian financial crisis of 2008 (Baumeister and Kilian, 2015). Recently in 2014, crude oil prices fell sharply after reaching monthly peaks of $112 (Baumeister and Kilian, 2016).

Currently, we are facing the biggest oil price drop since the Gulf War in 1991. The unexpectedly sharp drop in oil demand toward COVID-19 led to the dramatical falling of price on March 12, 2020 (OPEC, 2020a). The current drop in oil demand is caused by the quarantine of countries, particularly travel restrictions and containment measures. Indeed, an oil price war took place between Russia and the Saudi-led Organization of Petroleum Exporting Countries (OPEC). OPEC wanted to slash production quotas, while Russia, refused it, to undermine the extraction of shale oil in the United States. According to Rosneft, which is a Russian state-owned company specialized in the extraction, processing, and distribution of petroleum, if Russia would have accepted a drop in oil production to maintain the price, American shale oil would have found takers on the world energy market, that would not have been favorable for the flow of Russian oil. However, Saudi Arabia and Russia failed to reach an agreement on production cuts, which exacerbated the crisis (OPEC, 2020b).

Consequently, the price of U.S. crude oil was fluctuating just around $30 per barrel, it dropped from $150 per barrel in 2014 to $30 in 2020 (Alkhathlan *et al.*, 2014). Therefore, the unexpected price drop is generating high uncertainty, fears, and doubt. It turns out that many factors influence crude oil prices, such as the current health crisis caused by coronavirus outspread, uncertainty, economic news, overall supplies, consumer demand, and speculators and hedgers' behavior. In fact, the oil supplies, which affect oil prices, are controlled by the OPEC (Kaufmann *et al.*, 2008). They are also determined to use the new technology that allows extracting oil from rock, called shale oil, which allowed the US to become the world's largest producer of oil in 2018 and a major source of global oil supplies (Frondel and Horvarth, 2019).

Presumably, the oil demand fell sharply as a result of the global COVID-19 pandemic (OPEC, 2020b). In December 2019, a virus designed as a severe acute respiratory syndrome (SARS) was first diffused in Wuhan, a Chinese city. The infected cases increased to 27, on December 15, and reached 60 in five days. It was identified as a viral zoonotic disease later named the coronavirus (COVID-19) that spread quickly in China and was declared, on January 30, 2020, as being a public health emergency of international concern, causing 811 deaths among 3373 confirmed cases, on February 8, 2019 (WHO, 2020).

Unfortunately, the coronavirus has, speedily, emerged as an alarming contagious disease increasing dramatically the number of deaths, which required rigorous containment measures around the world. On March 11, 2020, the epidemic was qualified as a pandemic by the WHO (2020). Among other causes of the worldwide spread of the coronavirus, the world faced a sudden slowdown in the global economy, border closures, and a stock market crash on March 12, 2020, due essentially to the failure of negotiations of OPEC to reach a production quotas agreement. Around the world, the warm weather slowed down the spread of the coronavirus. In no time, countries were relaxing border closures and containment measures, which led to a resurgence in infected cases after successfully slowing outbreaks during the first wave.

Although there is a vast commodity market literature, the consequence of the health crisis on the energy market has recently become a topic of interest (Kakali and Kriti, 2020; Belaid *et al.*, 2020; Aloui *et al.*, 2020). By using the time-varying parameters structural VAR (TVP-SVAR) model, this study seeks to assess the COVID-19 shocks on the energy market during the first wave and to compare it to that of the second wave. We choose crude oil and natural gas as a proxy of the commodity market that is closely related to economic conjuncture. Crude oil and natural gas are widely used for diversification, hedging, and speculation (De Roon *et al.*, 2000; Gorton and Rouwenhorst, 2006). Hence, investors, speculators, and hedgers consider commodity markets as an instrument for hedging against the equity market risk (Gatfaoui, 2019).

The remainder of this chapter is organized as follows. Section 2 provides a related literature review. Section 3 introduces the methodology and the model investigating the effect of coronavirus on crude oil and natural gas price. Section 4 presents data and discusses the estimation results. In Section 5, we draw the main conclusions.

2.   Related Literature

As a component of derivatives markets, the futures market allows economic agents to hedge themselves against price risk. According to behavior theory, it turns out that investors' sentiment can influence oil prices. Thus, when they anticipate a decrease in oil demand in the future, investors may short-sell oil futures contracts, which leads to a dramatic drop in prices, implying that prices can depend on market psychology (Kaufmann and Ullman, 2009). The behavioral finance theory emphasizes the importance of psychology in the evolution of commodity market prices (Deaton and Laroque, 1992; Chambers and Bailey, 1996; Shiller, 2003).

Recently, the health crisis has become a topic of interest, for instance, Belaid *et al.* (2020) investigate the impact of COVID-19 on the domestic natural gas market in China and provide a sectoral decomposition of this effect. China, in order to lead well its energy transition (Li *et al.*, 2011) and to ensure a climate change with low CO_2 emissions, has increased the share of natural gas in its energy mix as it is considered a more efficient and cleaner fossil fuel energy compared to coal and petroleum. They found an increase in gas household consumption due to containment accompanied by a sharp fall in industrial gas consumption.

However, the growth in natural gas demand in China experienced a significant drop during the first trimester in 2020 due to COVID-19, and the decreased demand for industrial gas was not fully offset by increased gas household demand. According to Belaid *et al.* (2020), understanding this impact allows better management of future crises and they recommend including the pandemic's risk when predicting gas demand in China.

Kakali and Kriti (2020) blame the sudden drop in oil prices to demand and supply shock following the outspread of coronavirus. They carried out a descriptive analysis seeking to understand factors influencing the energy market in India due to the COVID-19 outbreak, particularly, the impact of the pandemic on the oil sector and thermal and renewable electricity sectors. India is considered as the third-largest energy consumer in the world, after China and the USA, and its national production is diversified between domestic resources and importation. According to Kakali and Kriti (2020), it is interesting to understand how the Indian energy sector is linked with trade and the global economy and how the market reacts in times such as the coronavirus. Consequently, the Indian energy consumption fell due to the pandemic by 22.1% from March 18, 2020, until April 4, 2020. COVID-19 outbreak led to a new trend in the Indian oil market whose demand has dropped, generating a glut supply, which has led to a supply shock. The measures such as containment and closure of borders have disrupted the oil demand due to the decline in export and domestic demand for oil. Consequently, diesel consumption saw a decline of 24.3% in March 2020 as compared to March 2019. Besides, Fuel Consumption of Aviation declined by 32% in March 2020. Because of this oil imports fell to 225 million tonnes in 2020 against 227 million tonnes in 2019.

Therefore, it is interesting to study the dynamics of futures prices on energy market during this health crisis and to compare the impact of COVID-19 during the first wave to that during the second wave. This chapter discusses whether the health crisis of COVID-19 could affect crude oil and natural gas in futures markets similarly for the two waves of the coronavirus.

3. Methodology

Because of the rapid and unpredictable development of this health phenomenon, there have been structural changes in the commodity market, which will cause changes in investor behavior on oil prices at different times. For that reason, it is interesting to examine the time-varying effects of COVID-19 on commodity indices. Therefore, we opt for a structural VAR model with time-varying coefficients and stochastic volatility (TVP-SVAR model) developed by Primiceri (2005) and Del Negro and Primiceri (2015). This model allows us to compare variables' responses during different periods in order to capture their variation over time. The model can be expressed as follows:

$$Y_t = c_t + b_{1,t}Y_{t-1} + \cdots + b_{p,t}Y_{t-p} + u_t \qquad (1)$$

where Y_t is a vector composed of two dependent variables, namely: the S&P Goldman Sachs (GS) indices of Crude Oil and Natural Gas and a shock variable related to COVID-19. c_t is $n \times 1$ vector of the time-varying constant, $b_{p,t}$ is $n \times n$ matrix of coefficients varying over time and u_t is $n \times 1$ vector of structural innovations. They are normally distributed. The covariance variance matrix of the residues u_t, which varies over time, is presented as follows:

$$\Omega_t = A_t^{-1} H_t (A_t^{-1})' \tag{2}$$

where

$$H_t = \sum_t \sum_t {}' \tag{3}$$

$$\sum_t = \begin{bmatrix} \sigma_{1,t} & 0 & \cdots & 0 \\ 0 & \sigma_{2,t} & \ddots & \vdots \\ \vdots & \ddots & \ddots & 0 \\ 0 & \cdots & 0 & \sigma_{n,t} \end{bmatrix} \tag{4}$$

and

$$A_t = \begin{bmatrix} 1 & 0 & \cdots & 0 \\ \alpha_{21,t} & 1 & \ddots & \vdots \\ \vdots & \ddots & \ddots & 0 \\ \alpha_{n1,t} & \cdots & \alpha_{n1,t} & 1 \end{bmatrix} \tag{5}$$

This technique allows a structural shock to generate coefficients varying over time. Thus, we can capture the variation in the relationships between the variables in different periods. In the following, we estimate our model using the method of Primiceri (2005) and Del Negro and Primiceri (2015).

4. Data and Results

4.1. Data

The aim of this chapter is to analyze the impact of COVID-19 shocks on the energy futures market, in particular, we are trying to compare the responses to the two waves of the coronavirus. Thus, in order to measure the evolution of the pandemic, we use the percent of changes in total deaths per day. We use, also, the Crude Oil and Natural

Gas S&P GS indices as indicators of the energy futures market. The studied period covers 253 observations, from January 23, 2020, to October 1st, 2020. We assess the impact of a COVID-19 shock on the oil and natural gas futures price during three periods: (i) The first wave of the pandemic, (ii) From May 15 to August 29 and (iii) From August 29 to October 1, characterized by a return of the virus.

4.2. Results

4.2.1. *Stochastic volatility*

Figure 1 shows the stochastic volatility of the studied variable: the variation in COVID-19 deaths, S&P GS Commodity Index (GSCI) crude oil, and S&P GSCI natural gas. The figure reveals three crucial periods. The first one is during the first wave of the pandemic. This period was characterized by a sudden and very rapid worldwide spread of the virus accompanied by a significant increase in the number of deaths, especially in China, Italy, France, Spain, and the United States. During these first months of the studied period, the volatility curve of the GS crude oil index shows two peaks. The first peak of volatility is recorded in March and it is probably linked to the announcement of a global pandemic on March 11, 2020, and the stock market crash of March 12, 2020. The second peak of volatility appears in April when the spot prices of oil fell to their lowest level in history to reach negative prices. These events lead to the disruption of the energy futures market. The high volatility of the futures commodity market is linked to several key factors: High uncertainty, severe economic recession, and an unpredicted sharp drop in oil consumption in an oversupplied market. Thereafter, we note a reduction in volatility over the second period from May. Indeed, during the summer, the number of deaths stabilized, and the pandemic seemed to be under control in several countries such as France, Italy, and China. Gradually, countries began to open borders, to resume flights, and to recover industrial activity, which led to a gradual recovery in demand for oil.

During the second wave of the pandemic which began at the end of August, there is a very slight increase in the volatility of the oil index but remains at a moderate level compared to the first wave. This may be due to the following reasons: In the first wave, the

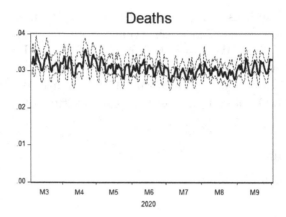

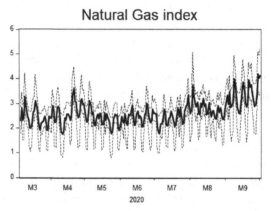

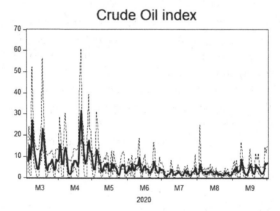

Figure 1:   The stochastic volatility.

sudden spread of the virus generated a disruption of expectations in the futures market. Although, during the second wave, economic actors anticipated the return of the pandemic. Thus, this second wave was taken into account in the expectations of investors and therefore in their decisions. In fact, stakeholders in the energy market were more vigilant and tried to avoid the collapse that occurred in March and April 2020. This enabled the energy market to resist and absorb the negative effect of the virus' return. The curve of the natural gas shows a slight fluctuation during the same period that remains moderate compared to the crude oil index. This owed to the fact that containment measures had increased the domestic use of natural gas. Thus, the negative impact of COVID-19 on natural gas during the first wave is less than that of the oil market. Then, we notice a gradual increase in volatility at the end of the studied period. This is probably due to the warm climate in this period, from April to September, where natural gas consumption is only linked to the industrial activity that is struggling to recover from this pandemic.

4.2.2. *Impulse responses*

Figure 2 shows the responses of the GSCI indices over 30 days to COVID-19 shocks. The effect of the shock remains for over 7 days after the shock before subsiding over time.

In the first wave of the pandemic, we notice a significant drop in the oil index of over 110%. Fundamental factors and financial factors explain the dynamics of the crude oil S&P GSCI in reaction to COVID-19. This health crisis led to a sudden economic recession, a sharp drop in energy demand in large countries such as China and United States, disagreements between OPEC and Russia, a sharp decline in dollar exchange rates, and a stock market crash. Those factors contributed to the collapsing of the oil market to reach negative prices.

During the second period from May 15 to August 28, 2020, a shock of variation in the number of deaths generated a drop of over 90% of the future index of crude oil and over 86% of the future index of natural gas. This period is characterized by slight stability in the number of deaths, the gradual relaxation of restrictions, and a progressive resumption of economic activity. In the third period,

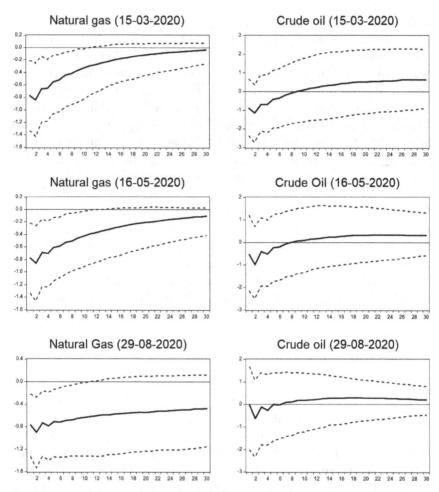

Figure 2: Impulse responses of Crude oil and Natural Gas futures indices to COVID-19 shocks on March 15, May 16, and August 29, 2020.

featured by the return of the virus with an increase in the number of deaths from the pandemic, a mortality shock generated a significant drop in both indices, especially, the natural gas index which recorded a drop of about 90% while the crude oil index only fell by 60%. Hence, during the last period, crude oil is still affected by the COVID-19 pandemic that continues to slow the recovery of economic activity. However, the magnitude of the response to the shock is less than that of the first wave. This result could be explained by the fact that the second wave was anticipated and expected by stock market investors.

The second reason is that, unlike the first half of 2020, in this second wave most of the countries have not carried out citizen containment and total lockdown. Governments are trying to fight against the spread of the virus by using other measures less costly for the economy such as distancing and wearing masks. These measures reduce the negative effects on oil consumption. In addition, China, the main trigger for the decline in oil consumption, has succeeded in containing the pandemic and is showing a moderate increase in mortality. Furthermore, OPEC as well as financial actors would be able to react quickly to avoid the April 2020 scenario, trying to contain and mitigate the damage. Nevertheless, the effect of COVID-19 on natural gas is getting worse with the second wave due to several factors. On the one hand, the demand for domestic natural gas is at a very low level during the summer. Besides, the drastic containment measures have halted the industrial activity. Thus, a hot climate accompanied by slow economic activity leads to a sharp drop in global natural gas demand. As a result, the storage capacity decreases rapidly to reach saturation leading to expensive storage prices. Furthermore, there is huge uncertainty as to the ability of the natural gas market to rebound in the coming months.

5. Conclusion

Using a TVP-SVAR with a stochastic volatility model, we compare the impact of the first wave of COVID-19 on the commodities futures market to that of the second wave. We show that impulse responses to COVID-19 shock change over time. The results show that the energy market is vulnerable to the surge in coronavirus deaths. It turns out that the pandemic continues to slow the recovery of economic activity and consumption. The results show also that the oil futures market was less damaged than during the first wave of the pandemic. The first one was sudden and unexpected, which upset all predictions and forecasts, while the second wave was anticipated, which reduced the effects on the futures market. During the second wave, stakeholders in the commodity market were poised to avoid the collapse that occurred in March. We find, also, that the effect on the natural gas market worsens over time and becomes severe with the onset of the second wave. These results come from the combination of many factors such as economic recession, expensive storage, warm climate, and enormous uncertainty. Finally, we can conclude that a significant recovery in demand for crude oil and natural gas may not happen until an effective vaccine is invented and distributed around the world. Mitigation and adaptation policies are crucial to overcoming the crisis. The commodity futures market will depend on the effectiveness of decision-makers' policies in containing the COVID-19 outbreak and reducing the negative effect of the global disease on economic activity.

References

Alkhathlan, K., Gately, D., and Javid, M. (2014). Analysis of Saudi Arabia's behavior within OPEC and the world oil market, *Energy Policy*, **64**, pp. 209–225.

Aloui, D., Goutte, S., Guesmi, K., and Hchaichi, R. (2020). COVID-19's impact on crude oil and natural gas S&P GS indexes. Available at SSRN 3587740.

Baumeister, C. and Kilian, L. (2015). Forty years of oil price fluctuations: Why the price of oil may still surprise us (No. 525). CFS Working Paper Series.

Baumeister, C. and Kilian, L. (2016). Understanding the decline in the price of oil since June 2014, *Journal of the Association of Environmental and Resource Economists*, **3**(1), pp. 131–158.

Belaid, F., Youssef, A. B., Chiao, B., and Guesmi, K. (2020, May). The Impacts of COVID-19 on China's. Domestic Natural Gas Market, IAEE Energy Forum COVID-19, Issue 2020, p. 108.

Chambers, M. J. and Bailey, R. E. (1996). A theory of commodity price fluctuations, *Journal of Political Economy*, **104**(5), pp. 924–957.

De Roon, F. A., Nijman, T. E., and Veld, C. (2000). Hedging pressure effects in futures markets, *The Journal of Finance*, **55**(3), pp. 1437–1456.

Deaton, A. and Laroque, G. (1992). On the behaviour of commodity prices, *The Review of Economic Studies*, **59**(1), pp. 1–23.

Del Negro, M. and Primiceri, G. E. (2015). Time-varying structural vector autoregressions and monetary policy: A corrigendum, *The Review of Economic Studies*, **82**(4), pp. 1342–1345.

Frondel, M. and Horvath, M. (2019). The us fracking boom: Impact on oil prices, *The Energy Journal*, **40**(4), pp. 191–205.

Gatfaoui, H. (2019). Diversifying portfolios of U.S. stocks with crude oil and natural gas: A regime-dependent optimization with several risk measures, *Energy Economics*, **80**, pp. 132–152.

Gorton, G. and Rouwenhorst, K. G. (2006). Facts and fantasies about commodity futures, *Financial Analysts Journal*, **62**(2), pp. 47–68.

Kakali, M. and Kriti, J. (2020). COVID-19: Demand and supply shock on 9 energy sector in India, IAEE Energy Forum COVID-19, Issue 2020, p. 77.

Kaufmann, R. K., Bradford, A., Belanger, L. H., Mclaughlin, J. P., and Miki, Y (2008). Determinants of OPEC production: Implications for OPEC behavior, *Energy Economics*, **30**(2), pp. 333–351.

Kaufmann, R. K. and Ullman, B. (2009). Oil prices, speculation, and fundamentals: Interpreting causal relations among spot and futures prices, *Energy Economics*, **31**(4), pp. 550–558.

Li, J., Dong, X., Shangguan, J., and Hook, M. (2011). Forecasting the growth of China's natural gas consumption, *Energy*, **36**(3), pp. 1380–1385.

OPEC (2020a). Organization for the petroleum exporting countries, Monthly Oil Market Reports, https://www.opec.org/opecweb/.

OPEC (2020b). Organization for the petroleum exporting countries, Organization for the Petroleum Exporting Countries, https://www.opec.org/opecweb/.

Primiceri, G. E. (2005). Time-varying structural vector autoregressions and monetary policy, *The Review of Economic Studies*, **72**(3), pp. 821–852.

Shiller, R. J. (2003). From efficient markets theory to behavioral finance, *Journal of Economic Perspectives*, **17**(1), pp. 83–104.

WHO (2020). World Health Organization, press conference on novel coronavirus outbreak, https://www.who.int/.

Chapter 7

Factors Influencing Electricity Consumption in the Containment Period: Evidence from the Residential Sector

Sihem Ben Saad[*], Aida Allaya[†], and Fayda Taârit[‡]

*Carthage Business School, University of Tunis Carthage,
Tunis, Tunisia*
Sihem.bensaad@utctunisie.com
†Aida.allaya@utctunisie.com
‡faydataarit@yahoo.fr

The health crisis following the spread of the coronavirus (COVID-19) around the world has had an unprecedented impact on the consumption behavior of consumers. The confinement has plunged the population into uncertainty and, for some, bewilderment. The purpose of this chapter is to examine the factors influencing electricity consumption of the residential sector during the COVID-19 outbreak. The containment measures that were introduced due to the COVID-19 had an impact on electricity consumption. Despite an overall decrease in electricity consumption, that of households has increased slightly. Several factors can influence this overconsumption. The constant presence of people in their homes and the implementation of teleworking imply an increase in household electricity consumption. In addition, the effect of confinement on households electricity consumption is influenced by a number of social, psychological, and cultural factors including the family size, children's age, social interactivity, flow state, lifestyle, and energy consumption culture. Other economic factors can influence the consumption behavior of households. Indeed, the massification of teleworking implies an increased use of computers and Internet networks. However, teleworking was not the main driver of variation in electricity consumption during containment, the use of cooking appliances also weighed the heaviest in the electricity bill of confined households.

Keywords: Consumption of Electricity, Behavior of Electricity Consumption, Social Interactivity, Flow State, Energy Consumption Culture, Life Style, Teleworking, De-globalization, Eating Habits

1. Introduction

In early January 2020, Chinese health authorities and the World Health Organization announced the discovery of a new coronavirus (COVID-19) linked to clustered cases of pneumonia that can be the cause of a wide range of diseases. By March 2020, COVID-19 shifted from being a Chinese problem into a global issue. With bleak growth prospects and low interest rates, the coronavirus has crippled the world economy. Response measures implied by this pandemic have impacted the economy of all countries through, for instance, reduced production, lower tax revenues, higher level of unemployment, increased government spending.[1]

In addition to its impact on economic activities, COVID-19 pandemic has also impact households' energy consumption. The containment measures led to a decrease in electricity consumption for businesses; however, households' consumption increased slightly. During the confinement period, companies were forced to substantially reduce or temporarily cease their activities. For example, in France and Great Britain, confinement led to a surge of electricity consumption at home by 3% (Statista, 2020). However, business electricity consumption in France was 15% lower than the level usually recorded in March. In the Tunisian context, the domestic demand for electricity production decreased by 4% during the month of March 2020 compared to March 2019. In addition, it recorded a remarkable decrease of nearly 28% on average during the confinement period

---

[1]See, among others, Boone (2020), McKibbin and Fernando (2020), Arezki and Nguyen (2020), Baldwin and Tomiura (2020), Beck (2020), Cecchetti and Schoenholtz (2020), Mann Catherine (2020), Cochrane (2020), Baker *et al.* (2020) and Albulescu (2020a,b), and Albulescu (2020c).

(Médianet,[2] 2020). However, for individuals, the containment has increased their electricity consumption.

According to Siècle Digital[3] (2020), Internet traffic has exploded by 70% worldwide through the frequent use of smartphones. Likewise, cooking appliances, streaming platforms, and online video games have seen more use than ever before, which has helped to increase household energy consumption. Another recent study by Statista[4] (2020) shows that the containment has had a significant impact on increasing the energy consumption of the user. What emerges from the study is the increase in web browsing by more than 70% of consumption in a few days. The television consumption also increased by 63%. With confinement, the use of social networks also increased by 61%.

WhatsApp has been the most used application during the lockdown period. It has recorded a sharp increase compared to the set of all social networks. Indeed, the application has registered a 40% increase in its use.

According to recent report by Statista (2020), the constant presence of households in their home and telework implementation have led to about 75% increase in electricity consumption within two months. Several factors contributed to this increase. Teleworking is among these factors. This is a particularly striking phenomenon of changes in organizations in times of confinement. Social psychological factors linked to consumer culture and economic factors have contributed to this increase. This chapter seeks to better understand the impact of these factors on household electricity consumption during the period of confinement.

The remainder of the chapter is organized as follows. We start by introducing the electric consumption behavior during confinement period. In Section 2, we discuss the explanatory factors of overconsumption of electricity. In Section 3, we examine the social psychological factors. In Section 4, we develop the factors related to culture, like lifestyle, psychology, and energy consumption culture. Section 5, we present the economic factors that may explain, also,

---

[2]https://www.medianet.tn/fr/.
[3]https://siecledigital.fr/.
[4]https://fr.statista.com/.

Figure 1:   Factors that influencing electricity consumption in confinement period.

this overconsumption (teleworking). Section 6 concludes. The factors that influence electricity consumption in the confinement period are presented in Fig. 1.

2.   The Behavior of Electricity Consumption During Confinement

The concept "electricity consumer behavior" can be defined in different ways. From a sociological and psychological point of view, the behavior of the electricity consumer refers to the electrical consumption activities of the electricity users and attitudes under the impact of external environments (Antonanzas Pozo-Vázquez *et al.*, 2017; Yang *et al.*, 2010). Due to business closures for coronavirus-linked lockdowns, there has been a major drop in the electricity consumption of businesses. For example, in France, the total average daily electricity consumption was 15% lower during the first two weeks of confinement compared to the previous two weeks (Statista, 2020).

The collapse in business electricity consumption is on average 25% in industry, 20% in the tertiary sector, and 13% in agriculture for the period from March 18 to 31 (Baldwin and Tomiura, 2020; Thorsten, 2020; Cecchetti and Schoenholtz, 2020; Mann Catherine, 2020). However, household electricity consumption increased by 4.5% over the same period. Several factors have contributed to this overconsumption. Teleworking, the use of digital leisure activities, and the need to use household appliances are among these factors.

During the confinement period, more intensive use than usual tends to increase household electricity consumption (Baker *et al.*, 2020; Albulescu, 2020a,b,c). Other factors can explain this overconsumption. In what follows, we develop socio-psychological factors, cultural factors, and economic factors.

3. Social Psychological Factors

Social psychological factors have attracted the interest of several researchers (Bressolles *et al.*, 2014; Balbo *et al.*, 2014; White *et al.*, 2014; Jamy, 2015; Zahao *et al.*, 2015). These factors refer to social interactivity, the presence of children, the need for social interaction, age, flow state, and number of family members.

3.1. The children and the need for social interaction

Children confined at home are an important factor that may explain the overconsumption of electricity (Susanti *et al.*, 2015; Cecchetti and Schoenholtz, 2020; Mann Catherine, 2020). Several studies have examined the relationship between the presence of children and the overconsumption of electricity. Two main streams of research present two opposing results. The first stream suggests that the composition of family members has a significant impact on electricity consumption. For example, Mcloughlin *et al.* (2012) studied the impact of the family with or without children on electricity consumption and found that the family that has children consumed more electricity than the childless family. However, Brounen *et al.* (2012) found that a family with more than one child consumes 1/5 more electricity than a family with one child.

Moreover, families with several children consume more electricity. Indeed, children tend to play on the computer, watch TV, and play games using electrical devices. These activities further increase the consumption of electricity. However, Bartiaux and Gram-Hanssen (2005) found that the child's age may explain the under-consumption or overconsumption of electricity. In an earlier paper, Cramer *et al.* (1985) found that children under three had no significant effect on household electricity consumption in the American family. However, for the family with children over 3-years of age, there was a significant impact on electricity consumption. Based on these findings, it is clear that children are an important factor in explaining electricity consumption during confinement.

3.2.   Age

Several studies show that age can influence household electricity consumption. According to (Yohanis *et al.*, 2008), electricity consumption is relatively high when the ages of the family members range from 50 to 65 years. However, electricity consumption is relatively lower when the ages of the family members is under 50 or over 65. Leahy and Lyons (2010) showed that in Ireland the electricity consumption of households where the family members' ages are between 45 and 64 was significantly higher than that of those aged 35 to 44. Mcloughlin *et al.* (2012) found that the power consumption of family household is lower when the members' age is 18 to 35 years. Kavousian *et al.* (2013) argue that in the United States, electricity consumption decreases when a family member's age is over 55 years old. To this end, we can see that the consumption of electricity differs according to age and culture.

3.3.   Number of family members

Several works have studied the relationship between the number of family members and electricity consumption (Bartiaux and Gram-Hanssen, 2005; Yohanis *et al.*, 2008); Leahy and Lyons, 2010). This stream of research suggests that the number of households can positively and significantly influence the consumption of electricity.

Electricity consumption will increase with the increasing number of households. The work of Leahy and Lyons (2010) and Rolland (2004) showed that an apartment shared by four or more people living together is likely to consume more electricity. Bartiaux and Gram-Hanssen (2005) studied the relationship between number of families, type of housing, and electricity consumption. The results indicate that the correlation between the number of households and the electricity consumption is the most important. Regardless of the types of housing (independent, semi-independent, or apartment), the number of households has always been associated with the consumption of electricity. Based on these findings, there is a positive relation between the number of family members and level of electricity consumption.

3.4.   Social interactivity

Interactivity is qualified as social because it refers to interpersonal interaction. Indeed, there is always a vital need for social interaction when an individual has been confined for extended periods such as due to COVID-19. The individual becomes extrovert, sociable, gregarious, talkative, and active (Eysenck, 1947).

Individuals who are rich in extraversion are hyperactive, show boldness, need company, place great importance on human and interpersonal relationships (Watson and Clark, 1997), and have a strong propensity to feel positive emotions (Rolland, 2004). However, studies have shown that introverts (individuals weak in extroversion) are rather calm, more socially isolated, and tend to avoid direct social contact (Rolland, 2004; Chittaranjan *et al.*, 2013; Meng *et al.*, 2014). To this end, we can argue that the need for social interaction has a significant impact on electricity consumption.

3.5.   The flow state

Research suggests the idea that the state of flow can have a significant impact on navigation time on the Internet and therefore the electricity consumption. State of flow is a psychological concept introduced by Csikszentmihalyi (1975). It is defined as a state of total immersion of individuals involved in a given activity such as internet browsing (Novak *et al.*, 2000). Several researchers suggest that the state of flow is characterized by a feeling of playfulness and total focus on a given activity (Novak *et al.*, 2000; Csikszentmihalyi, 1990; Ghani and Deshpande, 1994; Gharbi, 1998; Yadav *et al.*, 2013).

Other studies believe that the state of flow is determined by a sense of control and a perception of challenge (Gharbi, 1998; Novak *et al.*, 2000; Fornerino *et al.*, 2006). The state of flow is considered by many researchers as a central concept to explain more dependent variables, such as consumption intention and Internet browsing time (Ghani and Deshpande, 1994; Yadav *et al.*, 2013). The conclusions drawn are in agreement with those of Rosen *et al.* (2012) who believe that the feeling of flow is positively associated with Internet browsing time. Likewise, several studies have shown that the feelings of playfulness and joy are antecedent to the intentions of consumption (Bai *et al.*, 2010; Alalwan *et al.*, 2017). Rettie (2001) added the idea that the flow experience is positively related to the attitude and intention to play online. Therefore, it is possible that the flow is significantly associated with the consumption of electricity.

4.   Cultural Factors

These factors refer to lifestyle and energy consumption culture (Schipper, 1989; Angue and Mayrhofer, 2011).

4.1.   Lifestyle

The COVID-19 pandemic has shaken numerous well-established status quos including working styles and dynamics, lifestyles in the short- and long-term (especially social interaction), but also our consuming behaviors. In fact, it has been documented that both food and electricity consumption rose drastically during the containment.

The concept of lifestyle has been periodically addressed in relation to the social and behavioral aspects of energy consumption. Angue and Mayrhofer (2011) defined lifestyle as a model of culturally intelligible actions. Other research has defined that lifestyle does not only determine the mode of consumption but also includes, among others, the profession to be exercised, the equipment to be used, the number of children, the style ofpurchase (Angue and Mayrhofer, 2011; Schipper, 1989).

Despite the numerous social and anthropological differences from one society to another, the containment displayed similar trends and behaviors in most societies.

This includes comfort, which is a prominent factor in lifestyles. In the United States, a comfortable home should be heated in the winter and cooled in the summer, so that the temperature of a home remains relatively constant. On the other hand, the Swedish find that American houses are terribly heated, too cooled, and under ventilated.

As for the Japanese, they have a general resistance to heating and cooling of premises. Therefore, air conditioning is the first factor in electricity consumption, especially during the containment period. In addition, the consumption of electricity related to heating is strongly linked to the area of the house. Beyond the social and anthropological differences, a significant rise in energy consumption all over Europe was noticed during the containment period because of heating.

From Fig. 2, it can be noted that the electricity consumption during the heating-related confinement period has increased by 15% in Great Britain although temperatures are only 1°C different from March 2019. In Italy, full containment measures were put in place

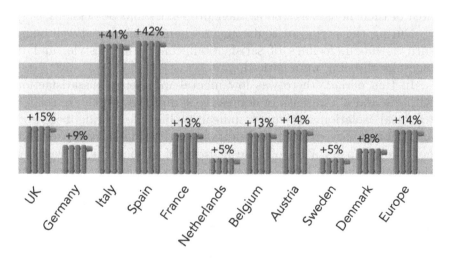

Figure 2:   Percent increase in home heating consumption.

Source: US Energy Information and Administration.

on March 9, but the use of heating increased by 41% throughout the month. Likewise, in Spain, the increase in the use of heating reached 42%.

Regardless of the weather conditions, the specific location of the home determines the level of heating use. In fact, homes that are exposed to the sun are warmer and use less electricity for heating. In addition, another factor that has determined the level of electricity consumption related to heating is the type of window that reduces heat transfer. Double-glazing and UPVC windows are important materials in reducing the consumption of electricity related to heating. The age of the building and the heating system also influence the consumption of electricity. The older the equipment, the more electricity it consumes.

The second major factor responsible for the amounts of electricity used during the lockdown period is the use of appliances, laptops, and televisions.

This lifestyle is highly dependent on household income and the number of households in the building. Lifestyle is strongly correlated with household income as it indicates how that income is consumed. Generally, rich people consume a lot of electricity because they have a high tendency to live in big houses. These wealthy people have less interest in saving electricity because they are not worried about the amount of their bill. This large consumption is strongly linked to the area of their houses as well as their properties and possessions.

During the period of confinement, changes in mental well-being such as mood, feelings of satisfaction, change in lifestyle, and in mental well-being were noticed.

In this period, there was low mental well-being, dissatisfaction with life and a high level of depressive symptoms, which are related to social isolation, sedentary unhealthy lifestyle, eating behavior, and poor quality of sleep. In addition, during the lockdown period, households spend a lot of time in front of an open refrigerator as their eating habits have changed; and stored a lot more food than usual. As a result, opening and closing refrigerators increase the electricity consumption of this appliance. According to IHS Markit, a Chinese database, the consumption of electricity in the residential sector increased by 2.4% during the 2 months of confinement. On the other hand, the use of new technology has increased by 27%.

During the lockdown period, electricity consumption increased and every day was a Sunday in terms of electricity consumption.

Changes in eating habits, psychological and emotional aspects amid social isolation imposed during the confinement period have increased electricity consumption in Italy. In fact, eating habits have changed. Italians said that during this period food was a comforting aid that reduced anxiety and stress. Some Italians said that cooking improved human relations between family members as they cook together. In addition, it stimulated the creativity of some people by elaborating new recipes (Di Renzo, 2020).

4.2.   Energy consumption culture

Energy consumption culture designates an interaction between cognitive norms, energy culture, and energy practices (Stephenson, 2010). The concept of energy culture is shaped by energy-consuming behavior that includes cognitive norms, energy practices, and material culture. In addition, this concept of energy cultivation is greatly influenced by external factors such as social level.

Figure 3 depicts the correlation between material culture, energy practices, and cognitive norms. As an example, the behavior of energy consumption related to electricity concerning home heating can be characterized in part by the values, aspirations, beliefs, construction style of the house, the presence of insulation, types of heaters and types of fuel, number of rooms heated, heat control settings, hours of heating use, and maintenance. Therefore, the interaction between material culture, cognitive norms, and energetic practices is strong.

For example, most New Zealanders have the choice of paying either a higher fixed daily rate with a smaller variable cost, or a smaller daily load and a higher load per kilowatt hour.

The first formula suits the households which have a higher consumption capacity and the second formula suits the households which have too much demand. Thus, the very large consumer and financially unstable user chooses an associated plan with a low fixed cost. Therefore, the pattern of electricity consumption is strongly linked to the interplay of standards, material culture, and practices.

Culture is defined by Hofstede (1980) as a collective mental programming, D'Iribarne (1993) defines it as a repository of meaning.

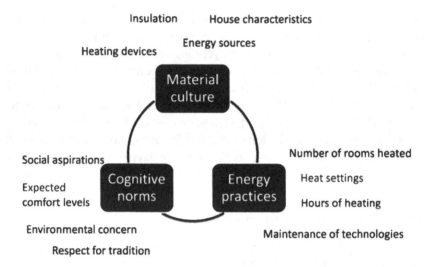

Figure 3:   Using the energy cultures framework to characterize some home heating behaviors.

Source: Cited by Stephenson (2010).

Culture can be considered as a frame of reference common to the same group of individuals which includes a set of standards and values influencing their actions and decisions (Dupuis, 2004). National culture offers a framework of understanding, specific to each nation, which is a function of factors such as languages, ethnicities, religious beliefs, and social norms (Angue and Mayrhofer, 2011). An individuals' culture reflects their energy practices, particularly in their consumption of electricity in the residential sector. Consequently, the national culture of households can affect their behavior and practices regarding the use of electricity.

Culture highlights the responsibility of households for the increasing consumption of electricity. Thus, during the confinement period, households perceive their home as a place of self-protection or healing and those who see their home as a friendly place to live are not particularly economical on a daily basis. Above all, they pursue objectives related to personal well-being and comfort. Therefore, during the confinement period, households seek to make their homes as functional as possible because it has become a friendly place and they do not seek to reduce their electricity consumption. Accordingly, in the period of containment, the consumption of electricity is a basic need that appears more essential as it is the only tool that allows us to hold on to the rest of the world in this period. It is thanks to energy that households are able to cook and store food; it is thanks to electricity that households recharge phones and stay in touch with their loved ones, but also to connect to the Internet and try to work and study as normally as possible or take advantage of video on demand services. On the other hand, economic factors such as teleworking and de-globalization may also explain the increase in electricity consumption by households during confinement.

5. Economic Factors

The containment measures that have been introduced to stop the spread of the pandemic have had an impact on energy consumption. As stated above, despite the overall decline in electricity consumption, household consumption has increased. It is difficult at the moment to determine all the effects that the coronavirus pandemic will have on the electricity sector. The conclusions drawn about the uses of electricity during the lockdown period differ from country to country. In fact, some households have reduced their uses while others have increased them (Gallego *et al.*, 2020). The permanent presence of members in the household will lead to a slight increase in consumption. This overconsumption can be explained by increased heating demand as well as additional use of household appliances. Indeed, there was a peak in consumption at lunchtime. On the other hand, surprisingly, the increased use of digital technologies (the Internet in the first place) does not seem to be the only major determinant in the evolution of electricity consumption (Abdi, 2020). In what follows, we discuss how economic factors (i.e., teleworking and de-globalization) have contributed to the increase in the consumption of electricity by households during the confinement period.

5.1. Teleworking

The rapid integration of information and communication technologies (ICT) within the professional environment has indeed changed the employment relationship, in particular by facilitating telecommuting (also called teleworking) (Bains, 1999). If working from home is considered a solution to the problems of urban congestion and pollution associated with transport, it is also recognized as the mode of work favoring a solution during the period of confinement. Indeed, containment is for some synonymous with teleworking (Montreuil and Lippel, 2003).

Teleworking, which has become essential to maintain part of the economy, generates additional costs for households. Because of the adverse effects of COVID-19 outbreak, many companies have made the wise decision to adopt teleworking in small or large doses. Indeed, since March, this has been the most recommended solution for their employees to stay safe.

While teleworking is not always possible for all jobs, it is at least for those who only require a computer and Internet access. The phenomenon of teleworking is the topic of numerous studies (Taskin and Gomez, 2015). It is considered to be the exercise of a professional activity in whole or in part, at a distance and by means of information and communication technologies. Indeed, the slowdown in economic activities as well as the constant presence of people in their homes necessitated the implementation of teleworking, thus resulting in a slight increase in household electricity consumption. This can result from the increased use of heating, cooking appliances, and the use of computers and Internet networks (Sim, 2020). If it is one of the safest solutions to continue to support part of the economy, teleworking does have a cost. Telephone connection or Internet subscription costs are not the only expenses attributable to teleworking. The consumption of heating, air conditioning and electricity are indeed taken into account, considered as "variable costs".

The increasing use of digital technology due to teleworking and confinement has thus led to an increase in the demand for electricity. But contrary to popular belief, the use of the Internet at home with teleworking is not the only factor responsible for this overconsumption.

5.2.   De-globalization

Today, no one can deny that globalization has been the greatest driver of development and wealth creation across the world (Rennen and Martens, 2003). The paralysis of economies, containment, and border closures shook demand to its core (**?**). One of the consequences of the coronavirus could be an abruption and the start of de-globalization. Too early to tell, but nothing will be the same again.

The first to have considered this process is the French President, Emmanuel Macron, after having noted, bitterly, that his country does not manufacture masks, or respirators, or even the active principles of drugs which are mostly manufactured in China and India.

Following the economic slowdown, de-globalization is driven by an aim to restore the growth of the national economy as quickly as possible; it is essentially a matter of relocating productive activity. All continents are affected by the crisis; Europe will inevitably be affected by the slowdown in the Chinese market, which has become one of the engines of global growth. German industry in particular, which is heavily dependent on Chinese auto buyers, is likely to be severely impacted. The United States is not immune either, for while it is aiming to resume the commercial and industrial conflict with China (Autor *et al.*, 2020), several countries across the whole world suffer from various and numerous shortages in every field.

In this context, households have discovered during shortages of drugs and protective equipment or even food that they now have to bake at home by themselves. The objective is therefore that of a rapid recovery, via a return to existing protection policies which also results in an increase in household consumption (e.g., making bibs, breathing apparatus, hand sanitizers). After the bib shortage period, most bibs are made in garment workshops. The households made the effort to make bibs at home and sell or distribute them for free and this is also one of the factors that increased the consumption of electricity during the confinement. In addition to masks and hydro alcoholic gel with the increasing number of severe cases flowing into hospitals, the demand for respirators is increasing. To address this issue, several respiratory masks have now been made by students with their own resources. The only real and viable solution would therefore be the relocation of part of the productive tool on the national territory. The coronavirus pandemic changes our view of globalization and shows that in certain sectors, supply difficulties can beget a strategic problem (Baker *et al.*, 2020).

6.   Conclusion

The economic situation, very complex in normal times, has become even more difficult with the COVID-19. The total containment of countries has not been without consequences on the international economy in general and on the consumption of energy and more particularly electricity. The health crisis caused by the coronavirus pandemic had unexpected effects on electricity consumption.

In fact, household electricity consumption during the period of confinement increased significantly. Staying at home and slowing economic activity have caused households to consume more electricity. Several factors of a psychological, social, cultural, and economic nature explain the consumption of electricity.

For instance, several studies have shown that the degree of electricity consumption is closely related to the age groups of the confined persons as well as to the number of family members. During the period of confinement the basic needs for social interactions increased and naturally the use of online communication means increased because the feeling of flow is positively associated with Internet browsing time.

With such a sudden change in lifestyle, the use of communication media and information technology has increased due to confinement, which at the same time is strongly linked to energy culture. We can say that the interaction between material culture, cognitive norms, and energetic practices is strongly linked.

The moment companies are forced to close their doors, workers are forced to work at home and consume more electricity than usual. In fact, teleworking has become compulsory during this period of confinement, but it was not the main factor in the variation in electricity consumption during confinement. De-globalization and relocation, which pushed home production, also account for the consumption of electricity.

References

Abdi, B. (2020). Coronavirus impact: Within ten days, 26 per cent fall in India's energy consumption. Retrieved from https://energy.econom ictimes.indiatimes.com/news/power/coronavirus-impact-within-ten-days-26-per-cent-fall-in-indias-energy-consumption/74854825.

Alalwan, A. A. *et al.* (2017). Factors influencing adoption of mobile banking by Jordanian bank customers: Extending UTAUT2 with trust. *International Journal of Information Management,* **37**(3), pp. 99–110.

Albulescu, C. (2020a). Coronavirus and financial volatility: 40 days of fasting and fear. Retrieved from https://hal.archives-ouvertes.fr/hal-02 501814.

Albulescu, C. (2020b). Do COVID-19 and crude oil prices drive the US economic policy uncertainty? Retrieved from https://hal.archives-ou vertes.fr/hal02509450.

Albulescu, C. (2020c). Coronavirus and oil price crash. Retrieved from https://hal.archives-ouvertes.fr/hal-02507184v2.

Angue, K. and Mayrhofer, U. (2011). La propension à nouer des partenariats internationaux en R&D: Une question de proximité ou de distance? *Revue Management International,* **15**(2), pp. 51–66.

Antonanzas Pozo-Vázquez, J. *et al.* (2017). The value of day-ahead forecasting for photovoltaics in the Spanish electricity market. *Solar Energy,* **158**, pp. 140–146.

Arezki, R. and Nguyen, H. (2020). Novel coronavirus hurts the Middle East and North Africa through many channels, Economics in the Time of COVID-19.

Autor, D. H. *et al.* (2020). The China Syndrome: Local labor market effects of import competition in the United States. *The American Economic Review,* **103**(6), pp. 2121–2168.

Bai, X. *et al.* (2010). Research on factors affecting mobile banking's using intention. *Scientific Decision Making,* **9**, pp. 14–21.

Bains, S. (1999). Servicing the media: Freelancing, teleworking and 'enterprising' careers. *New Technology, Work and Employment,* **14**(1), pp. 18–31.

Baker, S. *et al.* (2020). COVID-induced economic uncertainty and its consequences. Retrieved from https://voxeu.org/article/how-covid-19-t ransforming-world-economy.

Balbo, L. *et al.* (2014) Exploring the fit between justification and social distance in consumers' responses to online personalized recommendations. *32nd Advertising and Consumer Psychology Conference,* University San Diego.

Baldwin, R. and Tomiura, E. (2020). Thinking ahead about the trade impact of COVID-19. In: *Economics in the Time of COVID-19*, Eds. R. Baldwin and R. Weder di Mauro, CEPR Press, Geneva, pp. 59–73.

Bartiaux, F. and Gram-Hanssen, K. (2005). Socio-political factors influencing household electricity consumption: A comparison between Denmark and Belgium, Proceedings of the ECEEE, pp. 1313–1325.

Beck, T. H. (2020). Finance in the times of coronavirus, Economics in the Time of COVID-19.

Boone (2020). Tackling the fallout from COVID-19, Economics in the Time of COVID-19.

Bressolles, G. *et al.* (2014). A consumer typology based on e-service quality and e-satisfaction. *International Journal of Retailing and Consumer Services*, **20**(4), pp. 889–896.

Brounen, D. *et al.* (2012). Residential energy use and conservation: Economics and demographics. *European Economic Review*, **56**(5), pp. 931–945.

Cecchetti, G. S. and Schoenholtz, L. K. (2020). Contagion: Bank runs and COVID-19. In: *Economics in the Time of COVID-19*, Eds. R. Baldwin and B. Weder di Mauro, CEPR Press, Geneva, pp. 77–81.

Chittaranjan, G. *et al.* (2013). Mining large-scale smartphone data for personality studies. *Personal and Ubiquitous Computing*, **17**(3), pp. 433–450.

Cochrane, J. H. (2020). Coronavirus monetary policy, Economics in the Time of COVID-19.

Cramer, J. C. *et al.* (1985). Social and engineering determinants and their equity implications in residential electricity use. *Energy*, **10**(12), pp. 1283–1291.

Csikszentmihalyi, M. (1975). *Beyond Boredom and Anxiety*, San Francisco, CA: Jossey-Bass.

Csikszentmihalyi, M. (1990). *Flow: The Psychology of Optimal Experience*, New York: Harper and Row.

Di Renzo, L. (2020). Psychological Aspects and Eating Habits during COVID-19 Home Confinement: Results of EHLC-COVID-19, Italian Online Survey, Retrieved from doi: 10.3390/nu12072152.

D'Iribarne, PH. (1986). Vers une gestion culturelle des entreprises, *Annales des mines, Série gérer et comprendre*, pp. 28–39.

Dupuis, S., McAiney, C. A., Fortune, D., Ploeg, J., and Witt, L. de. (2014). Theoretical foundations guiding culture change: The work of the Partnerships in Dementia Care Alliance. *Dementia*, **15**(1), pp. 85–105. doi:10.1177/1471301213518935.

Eysenck, H. J. (1947). *Dimensions of Personality*, Oxford, England: Kegan Paul.

Fornerino, M. *et al.* (2006). Mesure de l'immersion dans une expérience de consommation: Premiers développements. *Actes du XXII ème Colloque international de l'Association Française du Marketing*, Nantes.

Gallego, V., Nishiura, H., Sah, R., and Rodriguez-Morales, A. J. (2020). The COVID-19 outbreak and implications for the Tokyo 2020 Summer Olympic Games, *Travel Medicine and Infectious Disease*, **34**, pp. 101604. doi:10.1016/j.tmaid.2020.101604.

Ghani, J. A. and Deshpande, P. (1994). Task characteristics and experience of optimal flow in human-computer interaction. *The Journal of Psychology*, **128**(4), pp. 381–391.

Gharbi, J. (1998). Les facteurs qui influencent les processus décisionnels des consommateurs lors d'un achat sur Internet. *Thèse de doctorat, Ecole de Hautes Etudes Commerciales affilié l'université de Montréal.*

Hebert, J. M. and Benbasat, A. (1994). Adopting information technology in hospitals: The relationship between attitudes/expectations and behavior. *Hospital & Health Services Administration*, **39**(3), pp. 369–383.

Hofstede, G. (1980). *Culture's Consequences: International Differences in Work-Related Values*, Beverly Hills, CA: Sage.

Jamy, L. (2015). The benefit of being physically present: A survey of experimental works comparing copresent robots, telepresent robots and virtual agents. *International Journal of Human-Computer Studies*, **20**(2), pp. 23–37.

Kavousian, A. *et al.* (2013). Determinants of residential consumption of electricity: Using smart meter data to examine the effect of climate, building characteristics, appliance stock, and occupants' behavior. *Energy*, **255**, pp. 184–194.

Mann Catherine, L. (2020). Real and financial lenses to assess the economic consequences of COVID-19. In: *Economics in the Time of COVID-19*, Eds. R. Baldwin and B. Weder di Mauro, CEPR Press, Geneva, pp. 81–87.

McKibbin, W. J. and Fernando, R. (2020). The Global Macroeconomic Impacts of COVID-19: Seven Scenarios. CAMA Working Paper No. 19/2020. Available at SSRN: https://ssrn.com/abstract=3547729.

Mcloughlin, F. *et al.* (2012). Characterizing domestic consumption of electricity patterns by dwelling and occupant socio-economic variables: An Irish case study. *Energy Build*, **48**(19), pp. 240–248.

Meng, G. *et al.* (2014). Analyzing the impact of proximity, location, and personality on smartphone usage. *Computational Social Networks*, **1**(6), pp. 293–298.

Montreuil, S. and Lippel, K. (2003). Telework and occupational health: A Quebec empirical study and regulatory implications. *Safety Science*, **41**, pp. 339–358.

Novak, Th. *et al.* (2000). Measuring the customer experience in online environments: A structural modeling approach. *Marketing Science*, **19**(1), pp. 22–42.

Leahy, E. and Lyons, S. (2010). Energy use and appliance ownership in Ireland. *Energy Policy*, **38**(8), pp. 4265–4279.

Rennen, W. and Martens, P. (2003). The globalisation timeline. *Integrated Assessment*, **4**(3), pp. 137–144.

Rettie, A. (2001). An exploration of flow during Internet use, Internet Research: Electronic Networking. *Application and Policy*, **11**(2), pp. 103–113.

Rolland, J. P. (2004). *L'évaluation de la personnalité. Le modèle en cinq facteurs*, Sprimont: Mardaga.

Rosen, P. *et al.* (2012). Social networking websites, personality ratings, and the organizational context: More than meets the eye? *Journal of Applied Social Psychology*, **16**(1), pp. 155–180.

Schipper, L. (1989). Linking lifestyles and energy use: A matter of time. *Annual Review of Energy*, **14**, pp. 273–320.

Sim, M. R. (2020). The COVID-19 pandemic: Major risks to healthcare and other workers on the front line. *Occupational and Environmental Medicine*, **77**, pp. 281–290.

Stephenson, J. (2010). Energy cultures: A framework for understanding energy behaviours. *Energy Policy*, **38**(10), pp. 6120–6129.

Susanti, L. *et al.* (2015). Demographic characteristics in correlation with household electricity use. *Industrial Engineering, Management Science and Applications*, **349**, pp. 959–968.

Taskin, E. and Gomez, D. (2015). Telework and mobile working: Analysis of its benefits and drawbacks. *International Journal of Work Innovation*, **1**(1), pp. 420–430.

Thorsten, B. (2020). Finance in the times of coronavirus. In: *Economics in the Time of COVID-19*, Eds. R. Baldwin and B. Weder di Mauro, CEPR Press, Geneva, pp. 73–77.

Watson, A. and Clark, B. (1997). Extraversion and its positive emotional core. In: *Handbook of Personality Psychology*, Eds. R. Hogan, J. A. Johnson, and S. R. Briggs, San Diego, CA, US: Academic Press, pp. 767–793.

White, T. *et al.* (2014). No strings attached: When giving it away versus making them pay leads to negative net benefit perceptions in online exchanges. *Journal of Interactive Marketing*, **9**(1), pp. 96–121.

Yadav, M. S. *et al.* (2013). Social commerce: A contingency framework for assessing marketing potential. *Journal of Interactive Marketing*, **27**(2), pp. 311–323.

Yang *et al.* (2020). Verification of deterministic solar forecasts, *Solar Energy*, **210**, pp. 20–37.

Yohanis, Y. G. *et al.* (2008). Real-life energy use in the UK: How occupancy and dwelling characteristics affect domestic electricity use. *Energy Build*, **40**(6), pp. 1053–1059.

Zahao, D. *et al.* (2015). Moving attractive virtual agent improves interpersonal coordination stability. *Human Movement Science*, **20**(2), pp. 240–254, http://www.sciencedirect.com/science/article/pii/S016 7945715000548-af005.

Index

Printed in the United States
by Baker & Taylor Publisher Services